SYSTEMATIC CHAMPIONSHIP WRESTLING

By the Same Author

Principles of Championship Wrestling (*With Buel R. Patterson*)

SYSTEMATIC CHAMPIONSHIP WRESTLING

Ray F. Carson, Jr.

SOUTH BRUNSWICK AND NEW YORK: A. S. BARNES AND CO.
LONDON: THOMAS YOSELOFF LTD

© 1973 by A. S. Barnes and Co., Inc.

A. S. Barnes and Co., Inc.
Cranbury, New Jersey 08512

Thomas Yoseloff Ltd
108 New Bond Street
London W1Y OQX, England

Library of Congress Cataloging in Publication Data

Carson, Ray F.   1939–
   Systematic championship wrestling.

   Bibliography: p.
   1. Wrestling. I. Title.
GV1195.C35   796.8′12   71–39347
ISBN 0-498-01140-2

Printed in the United States of America

To
mom and dad
whose personal sacrifices will be cherished forever.

Contents

Preface	11
Acknowledgments	13
Introduction	15

PART I WRESTLING PHILOSOPHY

1	A System of Wrestling	23
2	Criteria for the Selection of Escape and Reversal Techniques	26
3	Critical Analysis of Wrestling Techniques Employed in National Championships	29
4	Main Ingredient of Wrestling Champions	49

PART II COACHING METHODOLOGY

5	Organization of Practice Sessions	55
6	Unique Aids in Coaching	58
7	Basics of Scouting	66
8	Evaluating Wrestling Effort	69
9	Newer Approach to Wrestling Instruction	76

PART III TRAINING PHYSIOLOGY

10	The Science of Training	81
11	Interval-Circuit Wrestling	86
12	Strength Development for Wrestling	91
13	The Significance of Wrestling Endurance	95
14	Fartlek Training in Wrestling	101
15	Marathon, Sprint, Interval, and Repetition Training Applied to Wrestling	104

PART IV TAKEDOWNS

16	Coming to Grips	111
17	Major Weaknesses of Various Wrestling Stances	119
18	Upsetting an Opponent's Balance	125
19	Baiting an Opponent	143
20	Twisting Arm Fireman's Carry	151
21	The Bullfighter	158
22	Taking an Opponent Down from Behind	163

PART V ESCAPES AND REVERSALS

23	Why the Stand-Up is so Popular in Collegiate Wrestling	171
24	The Short Sit-Out: A Dangerous Wrestling Technique	180
25	Stand-Up with Hand Control	183
26	Standing Versus on the Mat Escapes and Reversals	194

27	Standing Chain Wrestling	206
28	Freeing the Hands	242
29	The Seven Most Effective Escape and Reversal Techniques Employed by N.C.A.A. Champions	254
30	The Long Versus the Short Sit-Out	264
31	Unusual Standing Escapes and Reversals	281

PART VI RIDES TO PINNING COMBINATIONS

32	Wrestle to Win	301
33	Waist Versus Ankle Rides	304
34	Principles of Leg Wrestling	311
Bibliography		324
Index		327

Preface

Ideas on strategy, mat tactics, drills, training regimens, and other crucial areas make this book an invaluable guide to winning wrestling. Novel concepts—far in advance of anything found in other texts of a similar nature—are its most distinguishing feature.

The author's many years of wrestling experience as a teacher, coach, athlete, and official have been compiled in new frontiers to this ancient sport. Intense research on national wrestling champions, covering a period of sixteen years, combined with the author's personal association with prominent coaches, provides the basis for many of the revolutionary concepts presented.

The book is ideally suited to meet the needs of coaches, those planning to become coaches, athletes, athletic directors, and physical education teachers.

It is unequaled as: (1) a textbook for undergraduate theory courses in coaching, (2) a reference source for beginning coaches, (3) a resource for experienced coaches wishing to improve their programs, and (4) an aid to physical education teachers and athletic directors interested in gaining a better understanding of the dimensions of the sport.

There are six sections to the book. Part I is an introduction to the theory of wrestling. An academic understanding of basic truths provides the foundation for a practical philosophy of wrestling based upon the cultivation of powers of discrimination.

Part II highlights fundamental principles of coaching. Coaching is presented as both an art and a science with only the latest and most prominent methods being discussed.

Part III concentrates on the scientific approach to training. Valid training methods are separated from those which are purely traditional. Emphasis is placed upon a complete, detailed description of unique innovative ideas in training.

Part IV discusses wrestling from the neutral standing position. Sound procedures are presented for taking down an opponent, based upon an analytical study of the strengths and weaknesses of various stances.

Part V is a presentation of findings of several years of research. Criteria, formulated from this research, are offered as a basis for selecting only superior escape and reversal techniques.

Part VI provides insight into determining which riding techniques are most effective. A basis for critically judging and evaluating the worth of various methods of maintaining control is provided.

As a whole, this book is a compilation of many of the author's published and unpublished writings. As such, a certain amount of duplication was inevitable. This was avoided wherever appropriate deletions could be made without jeopardizing the quality of the presentation.

Acknowledgments

There are many people without whose direct or indirect contributions this book possibly could have, but probably would not have been written. This group includes coaches, professional colleagues, and friends. Each of these people through some thought, word, or action stimulated the author's writing efforts.

Dr. Karl W. Bookwalter
Professor of Physical Education
Indiana University, Bloomington

Mr. Harry H. Broadbent
Wrestling Coach
San Diego State College, California

Dr. James E. Councilman
Professor of Physical Education
Indiana University, Bloomington

Dr. Thomas K. Cureton, Jr.
Former Director of Physical Fitness
   Research Laboratory
University of Illinois, Champaign

Dr. John B. Daugherty
Professor of Physical Education
Indiana University, Bloomington

Mr. Art Griffith
Former Wrestling Coach
Oklahoma State University, Oklahoma

Mr. Jess Hoke
Editor of *Amateur Wrestling News*
Oklahoma City, Oklahoma

Dr. C. O. Jackson
Head Emeritus of Physical Education
University of Illinois, Champaign

Dr. Harold E. Kenney
Professor of Physical Education
University of New Mexico, Albuquerque

Dr. John T. Powell
Professor of Physical Education
University of Guelph, Ontario, Canada

Dr. Kenneth G. Tillman
Professor of Physical Education
Trenton State College, New Jersey

Mr. Mark H. Whittleton
Wrestling Coach
San Diego City College, California

The author is especially grateful to Buel R. Patterson, former wrestling coach at the University of Illinois, for the ideas and concepts he shared so unselfishly and for many of the photographs used in this text.

Appreciation is also expressed to Herman L. Masin, Editor of *Scholastic Coach*, Gerald B. DeFries and Lanny W. Bryant, Co-Editors of *Scholastic Wrestling News* for their permissions to reprint selected articles.

Introduction

All too frequently, authors of wrestling texts are satisfied with presenting a proliferating description of how each technique is performed. They fail to aspire to an explanation of the intellectual, rational side of why certain movements comprising each of these techniques have to be performed as they are described in order for the desired results to be realized. Ed Onorato of Penn State University recognizes this glaring omission when he states (see article, "Wanted: Systematized Wrestling Techniques," in January 1970 *Scholastic Coach*):

> The last four or five years have seen a proliferation of books on wrestling techniques. Though welcomed by coaches, these texts leave much to be desired. They are little more than photo albums or dictionaries of moves; they don't proffer the kind of knowledge needed for intelligent coaching. . . .
> The books may be likened to coaching clinic lecturers who fail to explain WHY certain moves should be executed in a particular way. As a result, the new coach, looking for moves to teach, doesn't know which are suitable for him and which must be taught together in order to develop the needed continuity.

In general, little effort has been made in most texts to point out the "why" in addition to the "how" of wrestling. Since emphasis has been primarily in the area of "how," the attention of coaches has naturally been focused on the physical properties of performance with the "why" not being given the emphasis it deserves.

While there is scarcely any technique that does not succeed at least occasionally, many are nevertheless of doubtful value: they may work against beginners and weak opponents, but break down against stronger, more experienced foes. No wrestler equipped with an inadequate repertoire of skills can go anywhere in wrestling.

Most books explain only how particular techniques are performed. They fail to provide insight into the reasons for the discriminating ways the techniques are used. Very little can be gained toward the achievement of a sound wrestling program geared to producing champions if there is no practical explanation for the way in which the techniques must be executed.

The scholarly basis that bridges the existing gap between how wrestling skills are performed and why they are performed as suggested has only sparsely appeared in recent literature. This gap poses one of the most serious problems to successful coaching.

The contemporary coach is no longer solely an action-oriented individual interested in teaching only that which takes on the how-to syndrome. He is concerned about the "why" as well as the "how." His success in coaching is dependent upon the acquisition of understanding as well as knowledge. It is predicated on his ability to organize and conduct a well-planned wrestling program founded upon knowledges and understandings. Combining the how-to and why-of approaches to wrestling provides him with the insight necessary to facilitate foresight.

Knowledge may be defined as awareness or cognizance of information. This information concerns the details, facts, ideas, and truths that surround performance of a technique. Knowledge about "what" the technique is and "how" it is performed provides the basis for a primary level of intelligence. While essential to the higher orders of reason, this alone is inadequate for planning a sound wrestling program.

Intelligent coaching involves more than just this elementary knowledge. It requires understanding. Understanding denotes a higher mental process. It implies the ability to grasp the significance of this knowledge, to more fully realize relationships, and to apply discriminatory powers where they are concerned. It implies insight into existing relationships. They are aware of the significance of possessing more than basic knowledge. They do not accept knowledge as being terminal. Instead, they think beyond the "how" of something in order to more fully conceptualize the relationships and interrelationships that exist where none seemed to exist before. They cultivate the ability to recognize significant problems and work toward possible solutions. They are then able to make wise judgments and decisions based upon available information and interpreted within the scope of certain principles dependent upon a set of basic assumptions. In other words, the coach who attempts to explore and find answers to a multitude of questions is fulfilled in his efforts when he has developed the ability to reason.

Once this power to recognize relationships is possessed, the complex ability to judge the relevance of the various facets of problematic situations will develop. The ability to reason and understand provides the basis for solving these problems. The ability to separate the relevant from the irrelevant is invaluable to a coach; to do this, he needs to be equipped with something resembling a system of wrestling.

The tendency of texts to convey knowledge and knowledge alone is unfortunate since the development and progressive growth of the sport is dependent upon the conveyance and acquisition of understanding in addition to knowledge.

Until authors are willing to go beyond the "how-to" level of presentation and give reasons for why techniques are to be done in certain ways, wrestling will suffer. When they are willing to give the why-of-syndrome priority over the how-to-syndrome, something of significance will be gained in the pursuit of understanding the sport of wrestling in greater breadth and depth. Confusion will be dissolved and replaced by enlightenment. Inconsistencies will be pinpointed and eliminated. Bewilderment that accompanies ignorance will be alleviated. Action initiated with purpose rather than endeavors resulting from aimless floundering will be realized. These can and will occur once a concerted effort is made to write books that attempt to enlighten the reader through the conveyance of both knowledge and understanding rather than just knowledge alone. This is today's most crying need in wrestling.

This book is the beginning. It has been written for the purpose of conveying understanding. The contents provide insights into some of the fundamental ingredients necessary for conducting an intelligent wrestling program founded upon a technical application of both knowledge and understanding. It expands the present boundaries that have confined the potential of the sport of wrestling.

SYSTEMATIC CHAMPIONSHIP WRESTLING

Part I
WRESTLING PHILOSOPHY

1
A System of Wrestling

A COACH COMMONLY BECOMES RECOGNIZED AS SUCCESSFUL WHEN HIS team wins a conference championship or one of his athletes places first in the state finals. In either case, he receives a considerable amount of praise and a position of prestige among his professional peers. However, whether he was truly responsible for the quality of performance that resulted in this recognition is sometimes questionable. The team or the star athlete may have earned championship status in spite of rather than because of the coach's efforts. The supreme test is generally the consistency the coach has in producing champions.

The lack of a systematized body of techniques is the largest deterrent to a coach's success in producing consistent winners. The number of wrestling techniques reaches nearly 10,000. Such a large volume and variety frequently leaves a coach somewhat confused and bewildered. The number of possibilities is far in excess of what can either be taught to or learned by one individual.

A completely random selection of techniques would be foolish, since this would do little to prepare wrestlers for top-notch competition. Yet, in his attempts to make the best selection, a coach often flounders and ends up having to be satisfied with a hodgepodge of unrelated wrestling holds.

The question of which techniques yield the highest returns can be a difficult one to answer. Obviously, some techniques are superior to others. Each has a varying chance of success and failure. Of all the techniques that could be selected, each will be effective at least a percentage of the times it is employed. Some, however, can be executed successfully only against novice opponents of poor caliber. When attempted against stronger, more experienced foes, they prove to be ineffective. Others are of doubtful value. Their occasional success is overshadowed by the risk taken in losing points when they are countered. The chances of these techniques losing points for the wrestler attempting them are high.

A certain amount of discretion must be exercised in the selection of techniques. In order to fulfill his efforts to produce winning teams, the coach has to consider not only those techniques which have the greatest chance of gaining points, but also those which are the most likely to result in no points being lost if they are successfully countered.

The indiscrimante selection of techniques is avoided when a contemporary and comprehensive system is adopted. Such a system provides a basis for recognizing relationships among and between the factual elements in situations based upon observed and logical consistencies. It provides the means for judging the worth of any technique, prior to its acceptance or rejection.

A sound system of wrestling is founded upon the premise that there are criteria available for discriminating among the worth of various techniques. In order to make wise selections the performance aspects involved in the execution of each technique must be carefully studied and evaluated. The performance of any one requires the execution of a number of specific movements. The sum of these movements when put together comprises the total pattern of the particular technique. In executing each individual movement, the performer must place his body into various positions. A technique is only as good as the weakest position that must be assumed by the wrestler in order to properly execute the movements that make up the technique. No technique should be selected that requires the wrestler to make a movement that will make it necessary for his shoulders or scapula area to come into close or actual contact with the surface of the mat. The proximity of the shoulders to the mat's surface should be taken into consideration in the evaluation and final acceptance or rejection of each technique.

All techniques are distinct from one another and can therefore be classified into a hierarchical arrangement; such an arrangement separates those which are superior from the rest.

The poorest of all techniques are those which for proper execution require the wrestler to position himself—even momentarily—on his back. In this position, the wrestler is in the greatest danger of losing points or being pinned.

The next level of techniques of doubtful value are those which require the wrestler to assume a prone position. A wrestler on his stomach is half-pinned.

Next, are those techniques employed while the wrestler is lying on his side. In this position, a wrestler finds it very difficult to generate sufficient force to escape and is least able to resist a force applied perpendicular to the long axis of his body.

The fourth least desirable position is that of sitting on the buttocks—a precarious and unstable position. Once pulled or pushed to one side, it is difficult for a wrestler to return to a sitting position.

The next level of techniques necessitates the wrestler being on one or both knees. It is superior to the previous four, but is still of questionable merit. The weakness of this position is its lack of mobility. A wrestler on his knees cannot move very fast.

Rules are such that it is foolish to assume one of the above positions. Techniques employed from these positions are risky. Odds favor the wrestler who avoids them. For reasons of speed, conservation of energy, mobility, power, and economy of movement, a wrestler is wisest to work from a position on his feet.

The safest position is standing. While standing, the wrestler's scapula area is furthest from the mat. The further the shoulders are from the mat, the better are the chances of winning. While standing, the wrestler is more mobile than he is in any of the other aforementioned positions. He has only his own weight to support, which makes it possible for him to move faster than he could ever hope to do in any other position.

Techniques vary in their effectiveness. Those which do the most to enhance the chances of winning should be chosen. Making selections from among the thousands available can be simplified by the empirical application of certain criteria. Then a limited number of superior techniques can be placed into an ordered and meaningful system of wrestling. The system is founded upon the concept that techniques requiring movements which place the wrestler in a precarious position are inferior and should be avoided.

2
Criteria for the Selection of Escape and Reversal Techniques*

THE SUCCESS OF A WRESTLING TEAM DEPENDS LARGELY UPON THE COACH'S ability to select and teach effective escape and reversal techniques.

The common practice among coaches is to adopt the techniques which served them best as competitors. While most techniques will succeed once in a while, many are of doubtful value. They may work against beginners or poor opponents, but will break down against stronger more experienced foes. The indiscriminating coach often assumes the attitude that "IF IT WORKS USE IT."

The coach who is truly interested in getting the most from his investment in time and effort won't be satisfied with this philosophy. He recognizes that while most techniques will work part of the time, it is better to concentrate on the moves that will work effectively against the toughest of opponents.

Obviously, therefore, a certain amount of discretion is necessary in selecting techniques.

There is no shortage of opinions (in articles and books) about which escape and reversal techniques are most effective. The authors are fairly dogmatic about their beliefs. But all of them cannot be right, nor can all of their techniques be superior. Many of these authors fail to advance supporting evidence or reasons for the inclusion or omission of various techniques. Others often support their selections only by ambitious generalizations.

Unfortunately, much of the research findings have been contradictory. Perhaps it is this inconclusiveness which accounts for the lack of any sound bases in the selection of effective techniques. If no list of recommended techniques can be said to be completely accurate, none can be said to be completely wrong.

---

* This article reprinted with the permission of *Scholastic Coach*, January, 1970.

27 / ESCAPE AND REVERSAL TECHNIQUES

Several factors may account for these conflicting results in so much of the research. The investigators may be too superficial in their research observations; or perhaps, the variables of the techniques have not been related to the proper execution. I contend that valid criteria can be established by relating the height at which a technique is employed to the wrestler's position after an unsuccessful effort.

It is a well established fact that the most undesirable position for a wrestler is on his back. This position places him in the greatest danger of losing points or being pinned.

Most authorities will agree that the safest position is standing. That places the wrestler's scapula area furthest away from the mat. This may be the key to the whole problem of selecting techniques.

The following criteria may now be offered as a basis in selecting escape and reversal techniques. They are the body positions, in their order of importance, that the wrestler should AVOID assuming: (1) on the back, (2) on the stomach, (3) on the side, (4) on the buttocks, and (5) on one or both knees.

The coach should refer to these criteria in weighing all escape and reversal techniques. If a boy has to momentarily assume any one of these five positions in order to properly execute a technique, that technique should not be selected.

If one the other hand, the technique does not require the boy to place himself in one of these five positions, it should be considered a good maneuver and added to the teaching list. Though certain techniques can be employed from each of the five positions, none is preferable to something done from standing. This is simply a matter of percentages: the odds favor the wrestler working from standing. While points generally will be lost on a mistake made within one to four inches of the mat, few, if any, points will be lost on any mistake four feet above the mat. Once this set of criteria has been adopted, the following principles must be honored.

If broken down to his side or stomach, the wrestler should get back to all fours, free his legs and stand up. A wrestler who is flat on the mat is half-pinned. Once he escapes from his back to his stomach, he should recover to his knees and then to his feet.

The idea is to get on one's feet as soon as possible. The further the wrestler can keep his shoulders from the mat, the harder it will be for his opponent to score points.

In a standing position, the wrestler has two distinct advantages that he does not have while in any of the aforementioned five positions. First, he is more mobile. He has the ability to move fast. He has extended his capacity for maneuverability far beyond what it would be in any of the five "TO BE AVOIDED" positions.

The other advantage of the standing position is that he is carrying only his own weight and not that of his opponent. This assists him in moving faster and quicker while shifting his body weight and centering his balance to cope with the circumstances at hand.

The proper selection of techniques can prevent wrestlers from using maneuvers that can permanently impede their progress. The coach who maintains an attitude of "if it works use it" can justify almost any technique regardless of shortcomings, and he may wind up stunting the growth of some of his wrestlers.

Under pressure these wrestlers will turn to these ineffective moves again and again, regardless of failure. No boy equipped with such an inadequate repertoire of skills can go anywhere in wrestling. Coaches have a definite responsibility to teach the most effective techniques.

3
Critical Analysis of Wrestling Techniques Employed in National Championships

TEACHING THOSE TECHNIQUES WHICH HAVE THE GREATEST CHANCE OF gaining points while being least likely to lose points if successfully countered is a principal concern of wrestling coaches. The large number of possible techniques available has made selection one of the most difficult problems confronting a coach interested in constructing a sound wrestling program. A lack of adequate information has, in many instances, resulted in poor selections. While every technique is naturally effective part of the time it is employed, some result in the loss of more points than are gained.

Any coach suggesting the superiority of one technique over another has little to support the claim other than personal experience. Considerable disagreement exists as to which techniques are the most effective. Consequently, the author conducted a critical analysis of escape and reversal techniques in the hope that it might provide a starting point for agreement.

The need to establish a scientific base for the selection of wrestling techniques has been recognized by many past and current researchers. Within recent years, several studies have been conducted attempting to determine which wrestling techniques have been most successfully used by champions. Those techniques which were used most successfully were the ones which most often resulted in gaining points. All these studies, however, fail to take into account the effectiveness of the techniques—whether the wrestlers did or did not lose points when the techniques were unsuccessful. A technique was judged to be effective when it proved successful a great percentage of the times it was attempted. Little consideration was given to the percentage of attempts that resulted in no loss of points the times these successful techniques were countered.

Those techniques which had an equal percentage of success were in many cases vastly different in their relative effectiveness. The results of these previous studies are therefore of limited value.

A study of National Collegiate Athletic Association Championship Wrestling was conducted to provide more accurate information on the relative effectiveness of most escapes and reversals. The data collected were used to establish a basis for predicting which techniques could be employed with the greatest chance of success while at the same time providing the greatest assurance that they would result in no loss of points if unsuccessful.

This study focused attention on escape and reversal techniques employed in national wrestling championships. Films taken of national collegiate championships were viewed and data collected on a recording form similar to the following:

The recording form was kept as simple as possible so it could be easily understood and interpreted. Tally marks were placed opposite the appropriate techniques, and the technique was classified as a genuine attempt only if countered or successful. In this way, faking or feinting could be differentiated from bonafide attempts.

After the data were recorded, a cumulative frequency of attempts, according to categories, was compiled on each technique. These cumulative data were then organized and recorded onto the following graph according to rank and relative effectiveness. When the percentages of effectiveness of two techniques were identical, the technique with the larger percentage of attempts resulting in points being gained was considered the more effective.

Rank Order by Percent of Effectiveness of Escape and Reversal Techniques Employed During the National Championship Wrestling Matches

Escape or Reversal Technique	Rank	Percent Effective
Unclassifiable	1	91.7
Back-out	2	90.0
Leg-elevator	3	80.0
Power-house	4	79.2
Cross-body-scissors	5	73.0
Stand-up-whizzer	6	67.6
Sit-out-turn	7	67.0
Stand-up-turn	8	65.0
Inside-switch	9.5	62.5
Wrist-lock-lift	9.5	62.5
Shoulder-roll	11	62.3
Switch	12	60.6
Side-roll	13	59.5
Stand-up-roll	14	58.3
Stand-up-switch	15	58.2
Buck-away	16	58.0
Whizzer	17	56.6
Between-leg-pick-up	18	56.3
Step-over	19	55.5
Stand-up-shoulder-roll	20	55.0
Inside-side-roll	21	53.0
Bridge-back-scissors	22	50.0

31 / TECHNIQUES EMPLOYED IN NATIONAL CHAMPIONSHIPS

SCORE CARD FOR RECORDING DATA

Escape or Reversal Technique	Points Gained	Number Points Gained or Lost	Points Lost
Back-out			
Between-leg-pick-up			
Bridge-back-scissors			
Buck-away			
Cross-body-scissors			
Inside-side-roll			
Inside-switch			
Leg-elevator			
Power-house			
Shoulder-roll			
Side-roll			
Sit-out-turn			
Stand-up-roll			
Stand-up-shoulder-roll			
Stand-up-switch			
Stand-up-turn			
Stand-up-whizzer			
Step-over			
Switch			
Whizzer			
Wrist-lock-lift			
Unclassifiable			

33 / TECHNIQUES EMPLOYED IN NATIONAL CHAMPIONSHIPS

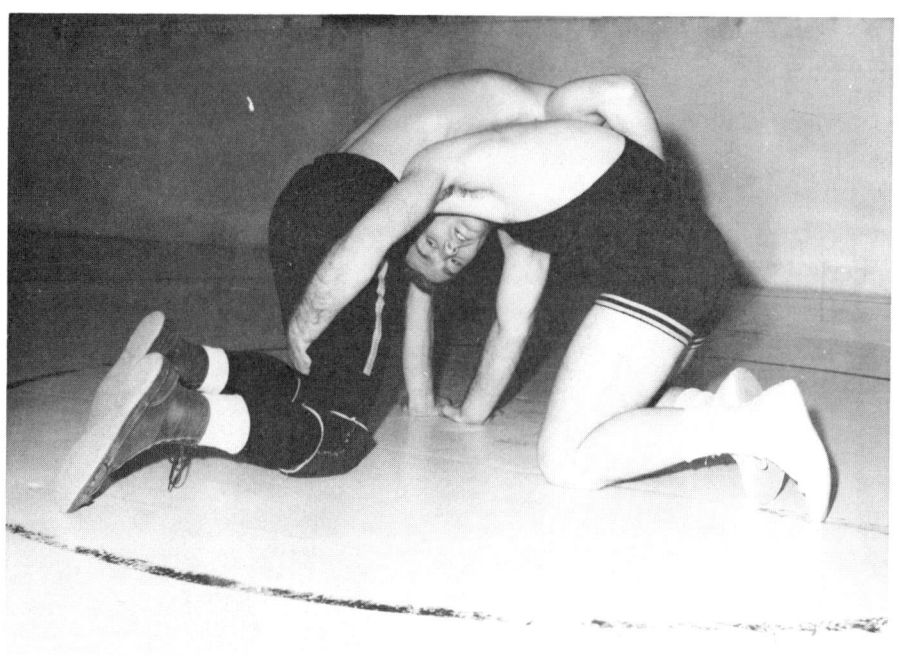

1A Back-Out

2A Between-Leg-Pick-Up

35 / TECHNIQUES EMPLOYED IN NATIONAL CHAMPIONSHIPS

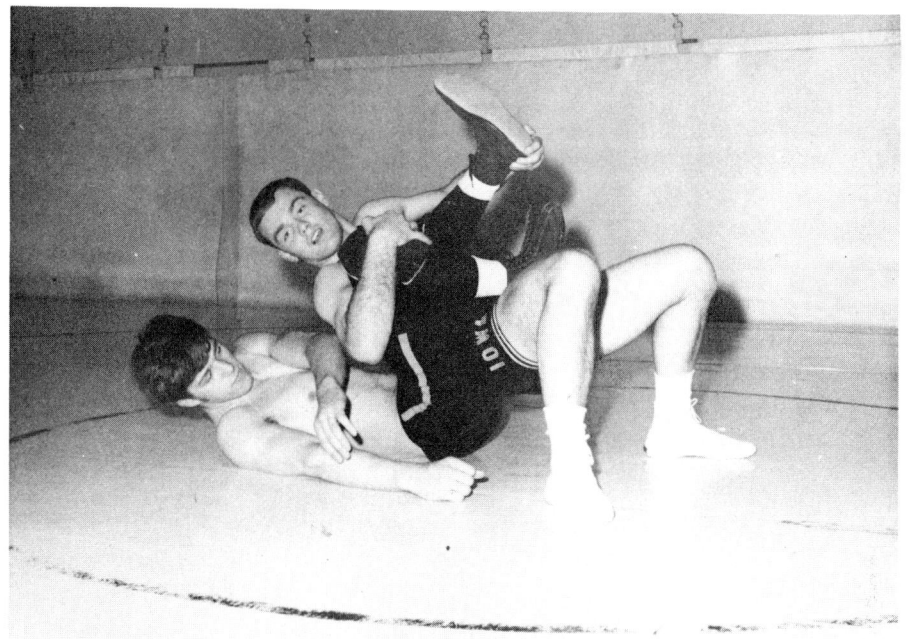

3A   Bridge-Back-Scissors

4A   Buck-Away

5A   Cross-Body-Scissors

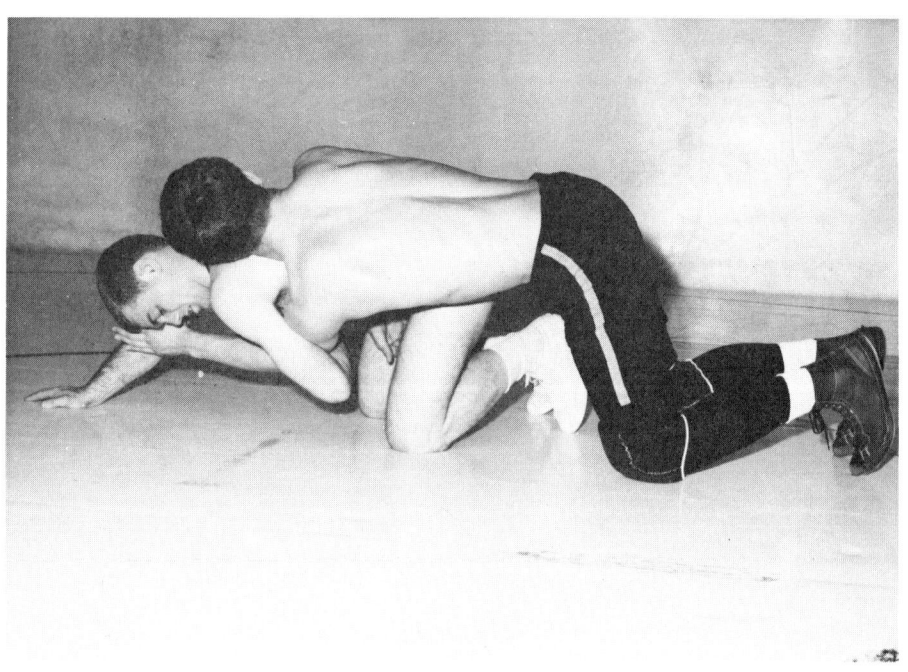

6A   Inside-Side-Roll

37 / TECHNIQUES EMPLOYED IN NATIONAL CHAMPIONSHIPS

7A   Inside-Switch

8A   Leg-Elevator

SYSTEMATIC CHAMPIONSHIP WRESTLING / 38

9A   Power House

10A   Shoulder-Roll

39 / TECHNIQUES EMPLOYED IN NATIONAL CHAMPIONSHIPS

11A   Side-Roll

12A   Sit-Out-Turn

13A Stand-Up-Roll

41 / TECHNIQUES EMPLOYED IN NATIONAL CHAMPIONSHIPS

14A   Stand-Up-Shoulder-Roll

15A Stand-Up-Switch

43 / TECHNIQUES EMPLOYED IN NATIONAL CHAMPIONSHIPS

16A Stand-Up-Turn

17A Stand-Up-Whizzer

18A Step-Over

45 / TECHNIQUES EMPLOYED IN NATIONAL CHAMPIONSHIPS

19A Switch

20A Whizzer

21A   Wrist-Lock-Lift

Twenty-one escape and reversal techniques were identified. Those which were executed from the defensive position and gained a neutral position were considered escapes while those which gained a position of advantage were considered reversals. Those which could not be recognized as any particular type of wrestling maneuver were tabulated as unclassified. Techniques which were dependent largely upon brute strength or upon some accidental advantage for success rather than scientific application were also listed as unclassifiable.

The graphic illustration ranks the most effective techniques as the back-out, leg-elevator, power-house, and cross-body-scissors in that order. The least effective technique was the inside-side-roll. It would be valuable to give instructional emphasis to these former techniques since they proved themselves to be highly effective when employed in championship competition.

Approximately 70 percent of the total number of attempted escape and reversal techniques was unsuccessful. Because such a limited percentage (30 percent) of the techniques was successful, it is important that the most effective ones be taught if the greatest benefit is to be derived from the time and effort invested.

The data, as presented in the following table, show the stand-up-turn to be the favorite technique used in championship matches. The sit-out-turn and the switch were the most popular techniques. This would suggest that perhaps more time should be devoted to practicing blocks and counters for these techniques. The data on this table also indicate that several of those escape and reversal techniques which were frequently attempted were less effective than many other techniques. Some of the more infrequently attempted techniques showed their effectiveness despite the fact that they were not employed often.

The step-over, inside-side-roll, whizzer, sit-out-turn, side-roll, and shoulder-roll were the techniques that resulted in the most points being lost by the defensive wrestler. Four of these techniques—the sit-out turn, shoulder-roll, inside-side-roll, and the side-roll—place the defensive wrestler in a precarious position in that they require for proper execution that the wrestler turn his scapula area to the mat. This would suggest that these skills need to be performed with the greatest caution since the risk of losing points is greater than with other techniques.

TABLE 1

Composite of Escape and Reversal Attempts Employed in National Wrestling Championships

Escape or Reversal Technique	Points Gained	Number Points Gained or Lost	Points Lost
Back-out	12	3	
Between-leg-pick-up	1	7	
Bridge-back-scissors		1	
Buck-away	8	42	
Cross-body-scissors	17	20	
Inside-side-roll	2	14	1
Inside-switch	3	9	
Leg-elevator	9	6	
Power-house	14	10	
Shoulder-roll	15	41	1
Side-roll	12	45	1
Sit-out-turn	66	101	7
Stand-up-roll	1	5	
Stand-up-shoulder-roll	1	9	
Stand-up-switch	11	56	
Stand-up-turn	179	412	1
Stand-up-whizzer	13	24	
Step-over	2	6	1
Switch	28	104	
Whizzer	12	53	3
Wrist-lock-lift	1	3	
Unclassifiable	45	9	

An important conclusion of this study was that the proximity of the defensive wrestler's scapula area to the mat, while executing an escape or reversal technique, was likely a determining factor in the attempts that resulted in points being lost when the technique was countered. It can be concluded that the best position from which to execute an escape or reversal was standing.

4
Main Ingredient of Wrestling Champions

MASTERY OF A LIMITED NUMBER OF TECHNIQUES, EXCELLENT PHYSICAL condition, and the will to win are the three qualities possessed by a champion. Of these, the will to win is, by far, the most important since it serves as the starting point for realization of the other two.

The will to win is characterized by a high degree of ambition and determination. It exists in a man who knows what he wants, possesses a burning desire to have it, and keeps trying until he achieves it. An aspiring purpose, an intensifying desire, and a sustaining persistence are the major sources of achievement.

PURPOSE

The goal is success. If desired keenly enough, nothing encountered will keep a man from acquiring it. A man with complete confidence in his ability to win, will win. Confidence is a prerequisite to success. With it a man feels at home on the mat. Not only does he know he is master of the situation, but he lets the opponent know it as well. From the very start he dominates the bout by compelling the opponent to wrestle according to his style. This places the opponent immediately on the defensive.

Believing in himself provides the self-assurance necessary for success. This belief is founded upon many hours of hard work spent on training and on perfecting techniques. When the time arrives for his efforts to be rewarded, he is mentally prepared to the point where he knows he cannot be beaten. He has developed an unquenchable thirst for success. He is success conscious. He is convinced he cannot be defeated. He is a champion, he perceives himself as a champion, and this concept follows him throughout his athletic career.

DESIRE

A good wrestler can never become a champion without desire. He may experience success, but never in abundance. There is a difference between wanting success and desiring it. Simply wanting, wishing, or hoping will not make it happen. Success demands a burning desire. It is the type of desire that is a keen, pulsating emotion which becomes more and more intense until it transcends everything else. It is this—and this alone—that creates within a man the feeling that he can be a champion.

Everything acquired in life begins in the form of desire. Success in wrestling is no exception. It is the type of desire that makes one willing to undergo months of intense training. It is the type of desire that requires willingness to subject oneself to a daily routine of burning lungs, anguished labored breathing, and the pain and agony that accompanies fatigued muscles.

Champions have insatiable appetites for hard work. They are so strongly motivated by their desire that they are capable of repeatedly pushing themselves into varying acute stages of exhaustion.

The difference between a champion and the rest is the champion's willingness to drive himself closer to his physiological limit. The rest have a natural reluctance to push themselves hard. The pain resulting from fatigue causes them to quit before they really have to. They operate up to their *psychological* limit but never truly approach their *physiological* maximum. Psychological rather than physiological factors determine the limits of their performance. The champion, however, narrows the gap between his psychological and physiological limits. He removes many of the mental influences that inhibit an all-out performance.

It takes hard work and determination to be a champion. Success is dependent upon being able to derive extreme pleasure from achievement. It is characterized by factors of motivation, pride, and a willingness to accept pain.

PERSISTENCE

Sustained effort is necessary to attain a goal. When the goal is success, effort must be backed up by a type of persistence that does not recognize failure. The goal must be held onto until it becomes a reality.

A champion never tells himself, "Ah, what's the use." Defeat to him is nothing more than a temporary setback. He learns from it. He is so success conscious and convinced that he won't lose that he doesn't.

A distinguishing characteristic of a champion is his hatred of losing. There is something in his makeup that will not allow him to accept defeat. He is convinced that winning is inevitable. He may concede that an opponent is an excellent athlete, but he never admits to himself, or others, that he might be defeated. He believes in himself and his ability to win.

Being success conscious makes defeat unlikely. Winning is attracted to the man whose mind is favorable to it and prepared to expect it. It provides the drive necessary to keep him trying no matter how hard the going may be. His willingness to put out to the limit of his ability keeps him from giving up. He wins by never quitting.

Once championship status has been attained, a reputation is established and has to be defended. The pride that accompanies this recognition then becomes the impetus for continued success.

CONCLUSION

The main ingredient of a champion is the will to win. Will power is a mixture of sureness of purpose, desire, and persistence. Knowing what is wanted, possessing the desire to do and to be, and having the determination to continue until that goal is realized provides the key to success. This concept is well expressed by Walter D. Wintle in the following:

It's All A State Of Mind

If you think you are beaten, you are,
If you think you dare not, you don't;
If you'd like to win, but think you can't,
It's almost a "cinch" you won't.
If you think you'll lose, you're lost,
For out in the world you find;
Success begins with a fellow's will,
It's all a state of mind.

For many a race is lost,
Ere even a step is run;
And many a coward fails,
Ere even his work's begun.
Think big, and your deeds will grow,
Think small and you'll fall behind;
Think that you can, and you will,
It's all a state of mind.

If you think you're outclassed, you are,
You've got to think high to rise;
You've got to be sure of yourself before,
You ever can win a prize.
Life's battles don't always go,
To the stronger or faster man;
But sooner or later the man who wins,
Is the one who thinks he can.

Part II
COACHING METHODOLOGY

5
Organization of Practice Sessions

WRESTLERS IN GENERAL ARE INCLINED TO FEEL THAT AFTER ATTEMPTING a new technique a few times they have mastered it. This is, of course, a false impression. The successful employment of any technique requires a considerable amount of practice before it can be executed instinctively at top speed. Ultimate success in using it is dependent upon proficiency. Yet, the repetition necessary to attain proficiency is oftentimes boring and extremely dull. Consequently, wrestlers are often more interested in "rasslin" and rolling around on the mat than they are in practicing techniques.

The solution to this dilemma oftentimes lies in investigating the manner in which the practice sessions are organized. Careful study of the organizational pattern of these sessions will frequently reveal inherent weaknesses. Methods of handling and conducting the workouts, if not actually producing the problem, may be aggravating it. Workouts that do not retain the interest of the athletes will do little to solve the problem. Unpopular drills, tedious exercises, monotonous routines, when conducted by an irritable, officious, bossy coach can only be expected to result in trouble. Routine drilling creates a situation where the soil is fertile for behavioral difficulties. Horseplay, mischief, and perhaps serious injury often are the end results.

Nagging, constant pleading, and commands given in a loud firm voice may correct the situation temporarily, but they do not solve the problem. An analysis of the workout session might reveal that it is basically a bore. This is especially true when it is handled carelessly, planned badly, and centered around activities that are insufferably dull.

The coach must be able to recognize the general symptoms of disinterest and heed the signals. Continuing with a boring activity will only result in ineffectual learning, substandard effort, and a desire on the part of the learner to fool around instead of practice.

The methodology used in first presenting a new technique should not include a complex description. Such an approach can be more harmful than helpful when a technique is initially being learned.

Early emphasis on details is undesirable. A general impression of how to perform the technique is all that is needed. Only the basic movement pattern required to perform the technique needs to be explained. At first, the only concern should be with the basic movements necessary to execute the total technique.

After the entire technique is demonstrated at the speed and in the manner it is expected to be performed when mastered, the learner should immediately be given the opportunity to try it. Additional guidance before the athlete performs the movement is of dubious value, because the athlete's initial interest is in trying to execute the maneuver. A few minutes of practice at the start is worth thirty minutes of explanation. Many mistakes will be eliminated by the wrestler himself as he readjusts his pattern of movement while attempting the technique.

Only after the general movement pattern has been learned should more details be introduced. Areas needing emphasis should be pointed out. Demonstrations on the mechanics of performing the technique should frequently be repeated.

Intermingling demonstrations and explanations with practice will diminish the boredom commonly associated with having to perform a new technique repeatedly. Repetition is necessary for mastery. Mastery is only acquired through practice.

Frequent meetings with the wrestlers provide the opportunity for presenting progressively more detailed instruction, and also provide an incentive to try the technique again. Motivation plays a large part in an individual's willingness to continue practicing something that could otherwise become dull.

The level of interest can be renewed and/or maintained by discussing common mistakes. Individuals having difficulty can be used as examples. Hints on correcting prevalent mistakes can be given.

During the times the technique is being practiced, individual instruction should be provided for those experiencing difficulties. When a common mistake is spotted, it should be brought to the attention of the entire group.

Wrestlers are often unaware of their mistakes. Demonstrating a mistake in slow motion, while they focus their attention upon it, is one of the best means of correcting it. At times, it is necessary to isolate that part of the technique which is causing the greatest difficulty. Overcorrection by repeated exaggeration of the proper movement is an effective method of eliminating the mistake.

Early in the season, most wrestlers look forward to practice. As time passes, however, enthusiasm often dwindles and boredom sets in. This may be observed in their weariness, lack of eagerness, and a loss of interest.

The monotony of the same type of workout day after day and week after week can create an attitude of restlessness, boredom, and inattention. Routine workouts can become wearying and sheer drudgery. Practicing techniques over and over can become an unpleasant experience and eventually a morale killer.

Proficiency can only be attained by repetition. Repetition, however, can be boring. Boredom can negate the benefits that would otherwise be realized.

Specific procedures can be employed to bring about a more positive attitude toward repetitive practice. Clever, creative, and ingenious ways can be devised to put a sugar coating on tedious work.

By introducing the element of competition into the practicing of techniques, interest can be maintained. Routine drills can be made more enjoyable by converting them into game situations.

Variety insures enthusiasm. The total time a technique is practiced, the pace at which it is practiced, and the amount of rest between each repeated effort are variables that can be manipulated. Occasionally, allowing individual wrestlers to plan their own workouts will alleviate a feeling of having to do the same old thing.

Procedures that distract from interest in practicing techniques should be avoided. Counters to a new technique, for example, should not be taught until a reasonable degree of proficiency in executing the technique has been attained. A counter taught before a technique is mastered will result in a loss of interest in practicing that technique.

Because of the nature of the sport, wrestling sessions tends to be hard repetitive work. If not properly planned, they can be extremely boring. Sessions that are interesting don't just happen; they are planned. They are characterized by varied, vital, and exciting activities. They are a result of a coach's willingness to dedicate time and energy toward making them a success.

6
Unique Aids in Coaching

TEACHING AIDS ARE NO LONGER A NOVELTY IN ATHLETICS. THEY ARE presently being used extensively in the preparation of athletes for high calibre performance. The reluctance, however, of some coaches to employ teaching aids stems from an opinion that they are difficult to operate and/or expensive.

In recent years, technological advances have made the operation of even the most highly sophisticated teaching devices relatively simple and uncomplicated. In most instances, it is quite difficult to make a mistake while using them.

Wrestling programs generally operate on very limited budgets. How the money is spent is a legitimate concern. However, while the cost of some teaching aids are prohibitive, others are quite reasonable.

Many aids can often be used without having to be purchased. Sources for acquiring them include rentals and loans. Departments such as audio-visual and physical education are oftentimes willing to allow their equipment to be borrowed. Aids commonly used by several departments or in more than one sport can be purchased from a combined budget.

One of the unique and most useful aids to coaching wrestling is the starting light. A highway flasher (photo 22A), commonly used as a warning signal in construction zones, is one of the most practical and inexpensive types of coaching aids.

Its irregular flashes serve as an ideal signal to begin wrestling. It is most useful during drills to insure continuous wrestling. Anytime a wrestler is pinned, collides with another, or goes off the mat, he can stop and start again on a predetermined number of flashes. The amount of time that would otherwise be taken up waiting for a whistle or verbal command is not wasted. It is also an excellent means of practicing starts from a referee's position.

A positive attitude toward practice does not happen by accident.

22A Starting Light

23A Phonograph

It is a direct result of careful planning.

A phonograph (photo 23A) can assist in evoking a positive frame of mind about enduring physical stress. It can make the wrestling room a pleasant area to work in and practice sessions more rewarding. It can increase team spirit and morale. It can get athletes mentally "up" for working hard. It can inspire them to execute techniques with greater enthusiasm.

Depending upon the response desired, the type of music selected that can act as either a catalyst in stimulating effort or as a pacifier in bringing about a more relaxed mood. Hard rock can elicit eager, aggressive, and invigorating efforts while softer, more soothing music can help relax tense athletes.

If the music is taped, a recorder (photo 24A) can also serve as a means of maintaining a running commentary at meets. Taping permits the coach to maintain constant visual contact with the action without having to shift his attention in taking notes. Following the meet, the tape can be played back as a means of evaluating the results. The tape is reusable after the information is no longer desired.

61 / UNIQUE AIDS IN COACHING

24A Tape Recorder

The most recent coaching aid developed for analyzing and improving skills is the instant video tape replay recorder (photo 25A). The recorder is equipped with a monitor and television camera for use in taking pictures with sound (photo 25B).

The major advantage of the video recorder is its instant replay quality. The time between the recorded performance and the availability of the tape is negligible. Instant replay makes the immediate appraisal of performance possible. The coach can point out deficiencies in the execution of various skills.

By seeing himself immediately after performing, the wrestler has instant feedback regarding his mistakes as well as his successes. He can see what he did wrong without having to question the coach. The reasons for the lack of success in competition can be studied and necessary corrections stressed.

25A Video Recorder

Both the tape and the film can be stored and replayed as much as desired. They can be erased repeatedly without loss in the quality of the recording.

Another rather recent coaching aid is the audible signal timer (photos 26A and 27A). This mechanical signal timer, in addition to being a valuable aid in conducting practice sessions in wrestling, is also useful in most other sports including football, basketball, track, and swimming.

Most signal timer units are activated and controlled by a button and/or audible sound. They are commonly employed as follows. A time interval is selected. At the desired interval a sound automatically repeats itself. Loud signals are sent out at the exact periodic times that the unit has been programmed for.

The benefits are noteworthy. The coach is freed from being a slave to a stopwatch. The boring routine of having to keep track of time is eliminated. An accurate account of repetitive work intervals is no longer in question.

The preciseness of the controlled time element is assured in conducting drills. Accurate timing of the exertion and recovery phases of

63 / UNIQUE AIDS IN COACHING

25B Video Monitor and Camera

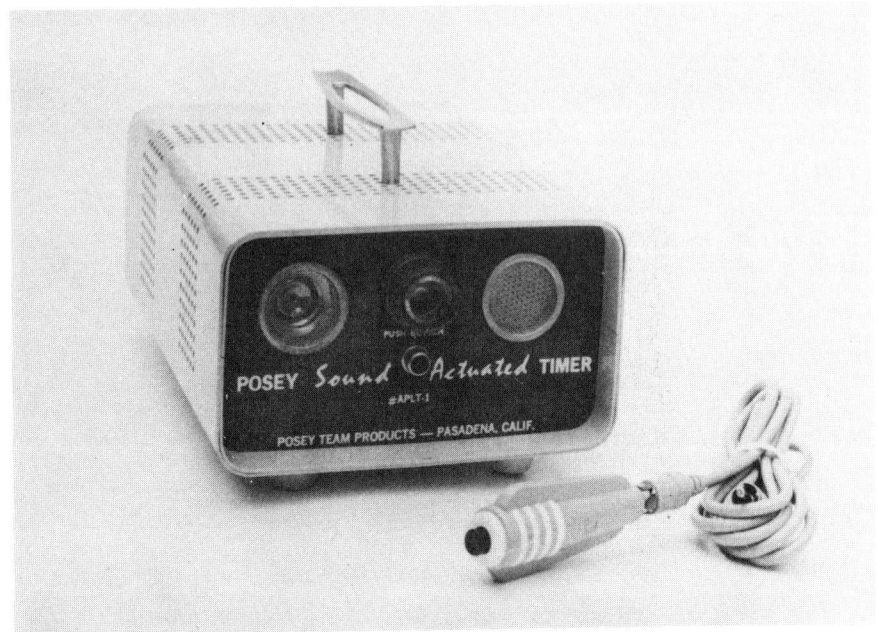

26A   Sound Actuated Timer

various types of training, such as interval, circuit, repetition, and so on, is guaranteed. This is essential for properly conducting a well-organized wrestling program.

In athletics, teaching aids are a necessity rather than a luxury. Many are available at a relatively inexpensive price. Due to the wide variety of available sources, price alone should not keep a coach from using them.

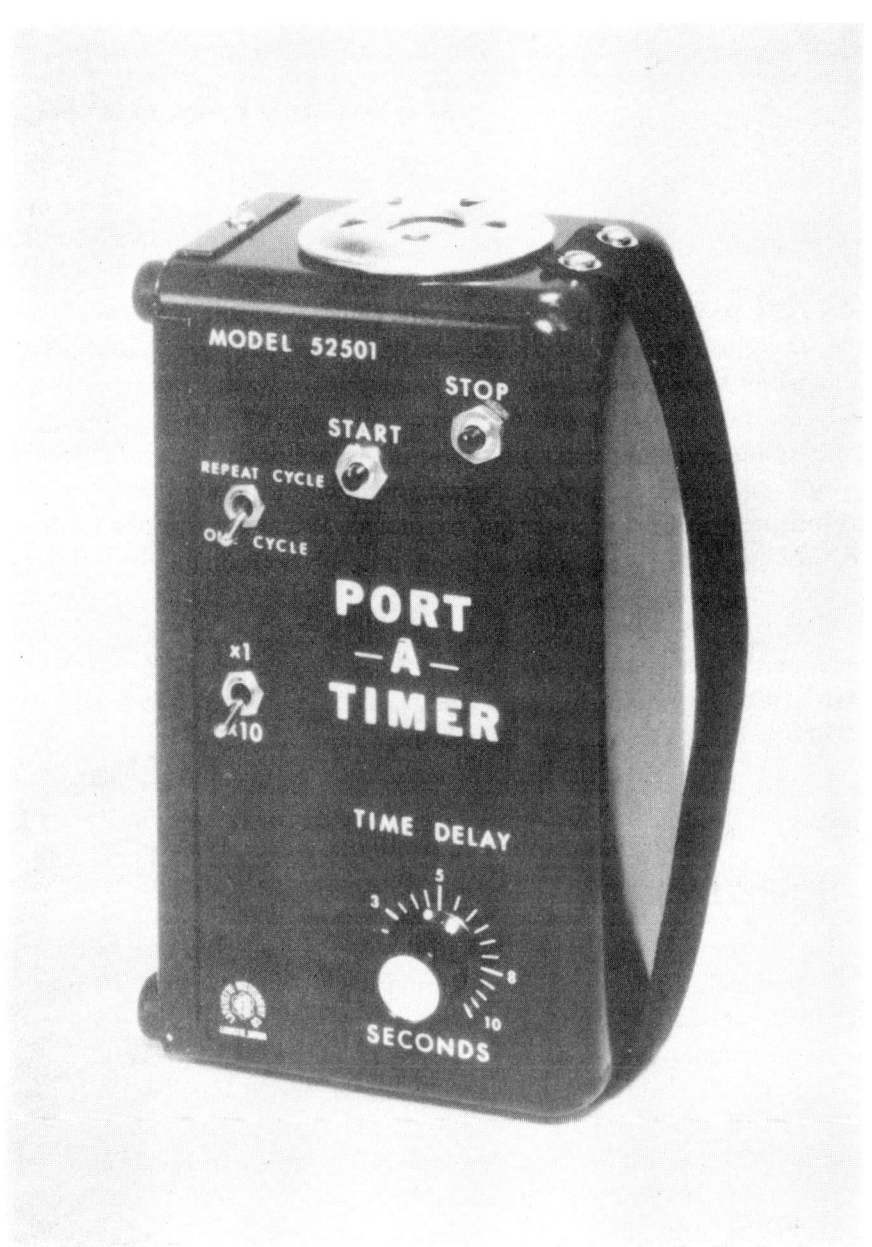

27A Audible Signal Timer

7
Basics of Scouting

SCOUTING MAY BE DEFINED AS OBSERVING, EVALUATING, AND RECORDING the strengths and weaknesses of future opponents. It is employed as an invaluable tool in all major sports. In wrestling, however, it is probably the most neglected aspect of coaching.

Scouting generally requires keeping a record of the techniques a future opponent popularly employs offensively and defensively. This record provides information that can be used in planning out strategy to take advantage of the opponent's weaknesses and thereby enhance the chances of defeating him.

Strategy requires taking into consideration both your own and your opponent's strong and weak points. Then by concentrating on one's own strengths and taking advantage of an opponent's weaknesses, success is more likely to be realized.

An objective review and evaluation of an upcoming opponent's strengths and weaknesses helps to establish immediate goals. Knowing what the opponent does well and what works well against him provides a profile for deciding what should be emphasized when competing against him.

This information provides the basis for focusing on moves to defeat the opponent. Practice sessions should accentuate techniques which are likely to be most successful. Considerable time should be dedicated to those techniques which have a favorable chance of success.

The typical scouting report form is often much too lengthy to be practical. It may contain more boxes and squares than a crossword puzzle. While trying to do a thorough job of filling in the blanks, the attention of the scout is constantly being shifted from the action to the scouting form and back to the action. Consequently, crucial phases of a meet are oftentimes not observed.

The author proposes to present a simpler, more concise, and more practical scouting form. It is a modification of one suggested by Art

67 / BASICS OF SCOUTING

Keith in his book *Complete Guide to Championship Wrestling*.

The proposed form provides a chronological account of all the moves tried during the progress of a match. It establishes a permanent record of the number and sequence of all attempted moves. It provides data on the success and failure of each of these moves.

A scoring key, amounting to a series of symbols, classifies each technique. A diagonal mark (/) is drawn through the symbol of any technique that is countered. As a means of identification, a circle is drawn around those techniques initiated by one of the wrestlers.

A discussion of the above recorded match will assist in gaining an understanding of how the scoring form is used.

In the first period, Brown had two double leg takedown attempts countered. This was the only action which took place during the first

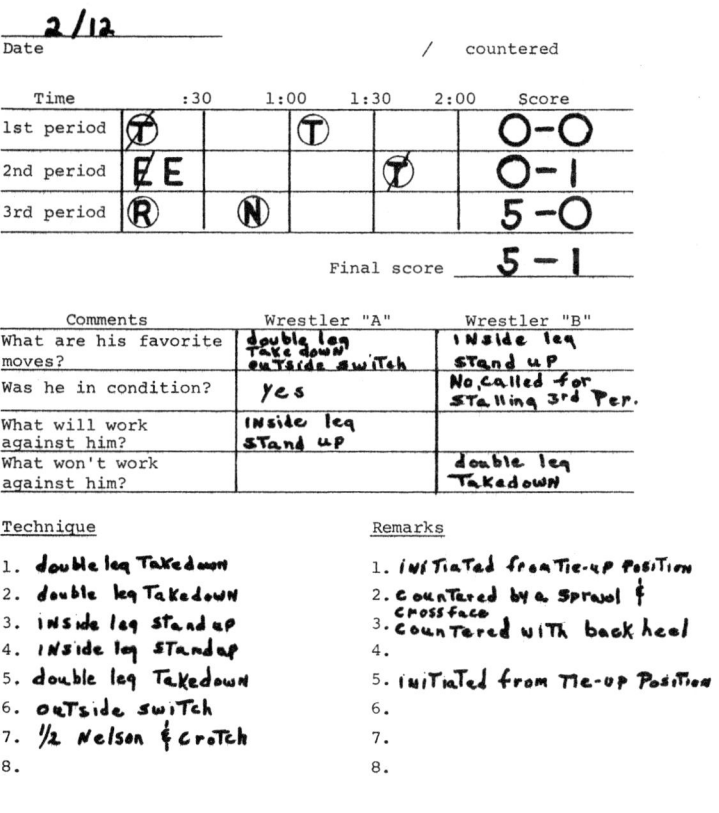

two minutes. The round ended with the score 0–0.

The second round started with Anderson being unsuccessful in attempting a stand up escape. A second similar attempt was, however, successful. Brown again had a double leg takedown countered. The score at the end of the second period was 1–0 in favor of Anderson.

Round three began by Brown successfully reversing Anderson with an outside switch. Later in the period Anderson was nearly pinned with a half-nelson and crotch combination. The third round was 0–5 for Brown. The final score was 1–5 with Brown being the winner.

In analyzing the progress of the match, it should be noted that all three attempts by Brown to take his opponent to the mat were double leg takedowns. All were initiated from a tie-up position. Although each was successfully countered, the particular technique was repeatedly attempted. Anderson did not attempt a takedown, although he effectively countered three attempts made by his opponent.

When Brown was on top he scored five points. On his first attempt to reverse his opponent, his outside switch was successful. He then went on to break Anderson down and score a near fall.

While working on top, Anderson was unable to score. In the bottom position, he attempted the stand up escape twice and was successful on the second attempt.

The scouting report provides a means of readily measuring both the strengths and weaknesses of both wrestlers. It is a sound basis for analyzing a future opponent's greatest vulnerability. This information should be used in designing a plan of action.

When an opponent wrestles according to the pattern suggested by the scouting report, he is more likely to be defeated. No greater satisfaction can be felt by a coach, team, or individual wrestler than when the planned strategy works as predicted.

8
Evaluating Wrestling Effort*

WRESTLING COACHES ARE CONSTANTLY PLAGUED WITH THE PROBLEM OF accurately evaluating their athletes' efforts during practices and matches. They have to rely on subjective assessment to determine the intensity of the effort.

Though a knowing coach usually can separate the loafers from the workers, subjective assessments involve a lot of guesswork; and whenever you have guesswork you must have errors.

What can the wrestling coach do about it? We recommend periodic checks of the heart rate. They offer a simple but precise means of evaluating the degree to which wrestlers are exerting themselves.

Several research studies have been made on the use of heart rates in assessing effort. Astrand, et al. indicate that the heart beats 110 times per minute at 40 percent of maximum effort and 186 times at 100 percent effort.

Karvonen suggests that positive changes in cardiovascular (heart) function are realized only when the heart rate indicates at least 70 percent of maximum effort.

These data make it possible to calculate heart rates in terms of working capacity. Suppose a wrestler's resting heart rate is known to be 60 beats per minute. His maximum heart rate, according to Astrand's study, is approximately 186 beats per minute. By applying the formula suggested by Karvonen, it is possible to determine how much effort the athlete must exert in order to make cardiovascular improvements.

(MAXIMUM HEART RATE − RESTING HEART RATE) × 70% + RESTING HEART RATE = EXERCISE HEART RATE

Example: Maximum heart rate = 186
Resting heart rate = 60

$$(186 - 60) \times 70\% + 60 = 148$$

* This article reprinted with the permission of *Scholastic Coach*, March 1971.

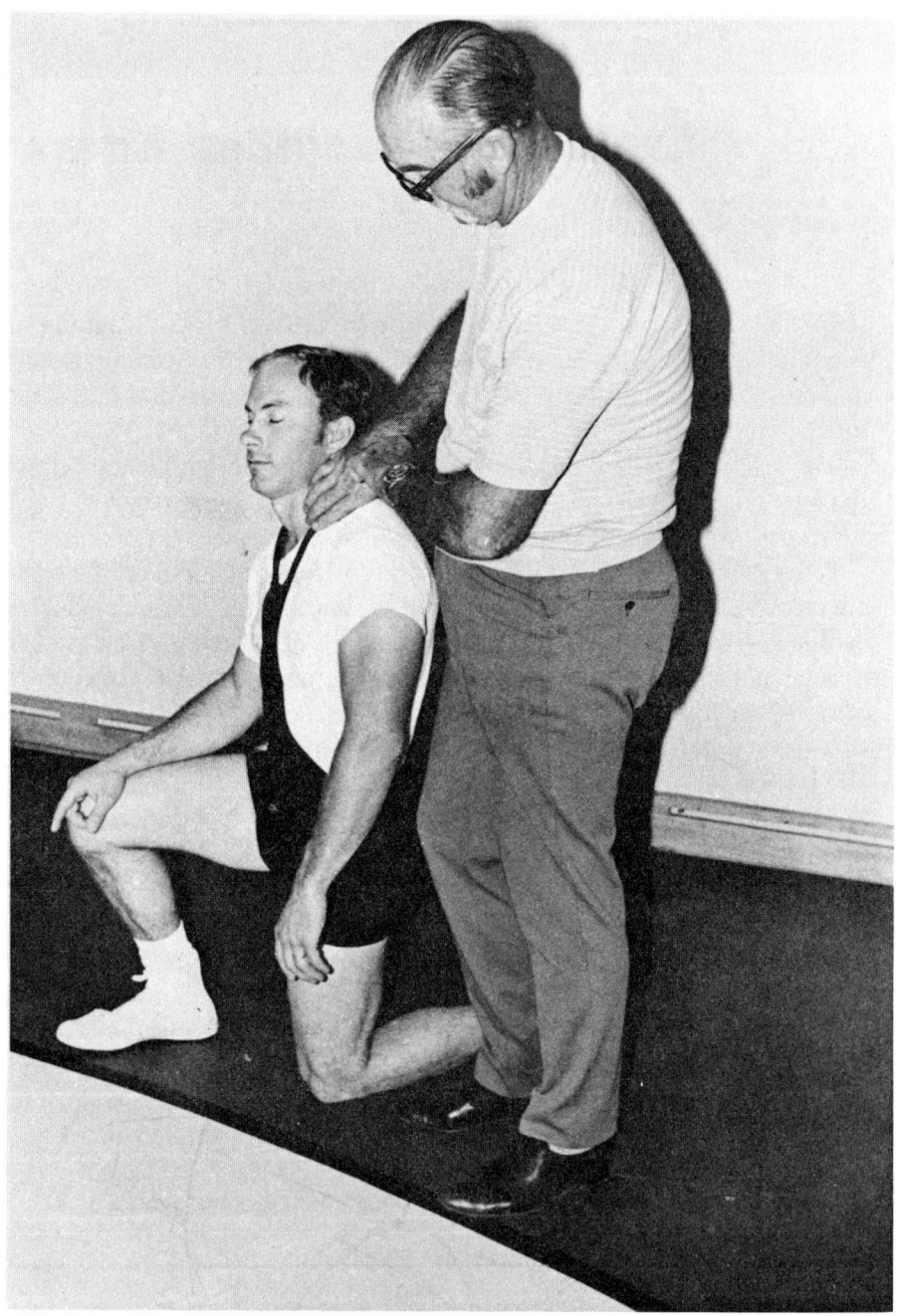

28A Checking the Pulse Rate

The figure 148 is the minimal heart rate or exercise level that the wrestler must reach and maintain in order to work at 70 percent effort. When his heart rate falls below 148 beats per minute, the pace of the exercise must be increased in order to improve cardiovascular function.

The actual amount of work done in a unit of time (intensity) will depend largely on the pace at which the wrestler performs. He can push himself or take it easy. Anytime the coach observes a loafer he should immediately check the wrestler's heart rate to corroborate his suspicion.

This can be done by pressing the fingertips lightly against the carotid artery located at either side of the neck (photo 28A).

A ten-second count of the beats multiplied by six provides the exercise heart rate per minute. For the wrestler's exercise heart rate to be approximately 148 beats per minute, the ten-second count must be 25 (25 beats/min. $\times$ 6 = 148 approx.).

Assuming that the wrestler's average resting heart rate is 60 beats/minute, the following table is useful:

HEART RATE AND WORK LEVEL

Percent Effort	Resting Heart Rate	Ten Second Count
0	60	10
10	73	12
20	85	14
30	98	16
40	110	18
50	123	20
60	135	23
70	148	25
80	160	27
90	172	29
100	186	31

The average conditioned athlete, exercising regularly, will have a resting heart rate of about 60 beats per minute or less. Heart rates vary considerably, however, since training tends to reduce the resting heart rate; it may therefore be advisable to check each wrestler periodically for possible changes.

Heart rate counts also can serve as motivators. The ability to determine heart rate can help individualize training efforts (photo 29A), thus encouraging the wrestler to work harder. The wise coach will, however, confirm the accuracy of the initial counts.

In using heart rate as a means of measuring effort, it is essential to understand the physiology involved. Heart rate is measured in beats

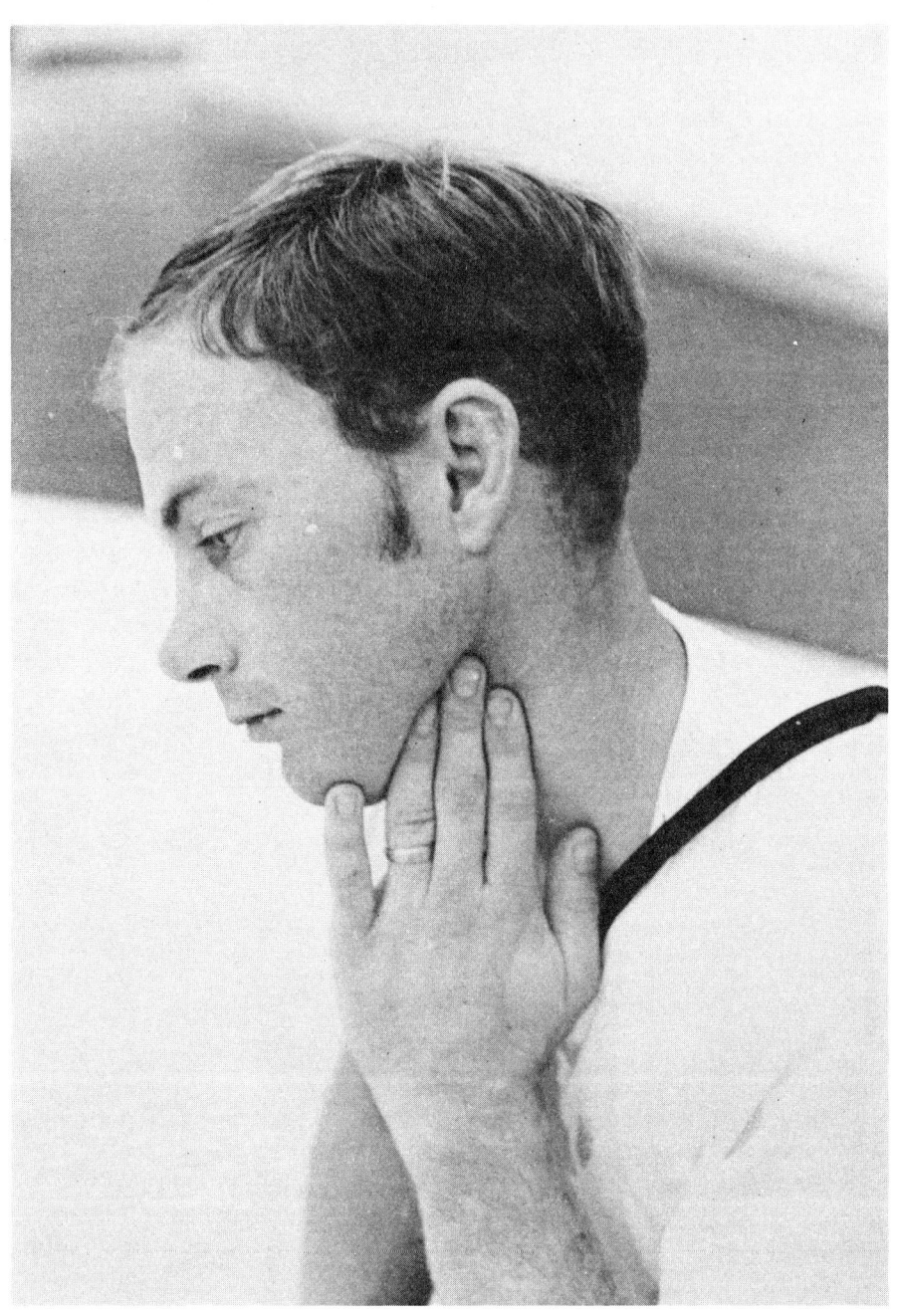

29A Counting the Pulse Rate

per minute. It increases in varying degrees, depending upon the intensity, duration, and type of activity.

With each beat the heart pumps or pushes blood into arteries. In the average athlete this occurs 60 times a minute. The arteries, which act somewhat like water pipes, carry blood to various parts of the body. The walls of the arteries are elastic. They stretch with each beat of the heart like a rubber band when it is pulled.

The blood, which is being forced into these arteries, causes the elastic arteries to stretch or bulge outward under its pressure. The diameter of the arteries thus increases as the blood is driven through, and contracts again once the current or flow of blood has surged past.

This bulging or pulse can be felt wherever an artery approaches the surface of the skin. During physical exercise, this is most notable at either side of the neck. If you place your fingertips just below the earlobe, you will feel the rise and fall of the carotid artery.

This rise and fall is the pulse. It is caused by the pumping of the heart and stretching of the artery. Only a slight pressure of the fingertips is required to feel and count each pulse. When counting the pulse, the checker should keep a watch or clock with a second hand in close view (photo 30A). The tips of the fingers are moved around slightly

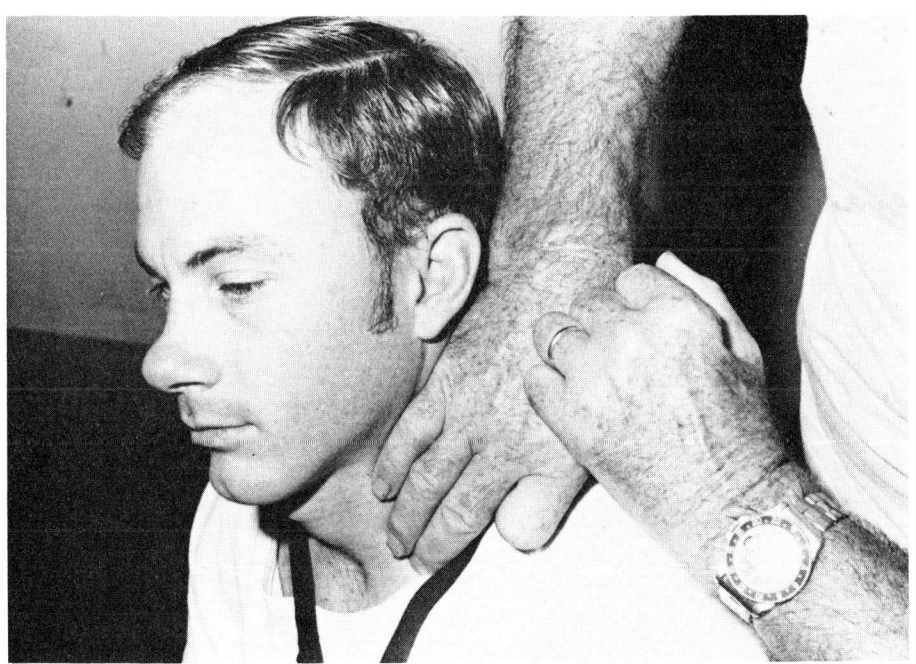

30A Timing the Pulse Rate

and the pressure varied until the pulse is detected. The pulse count is taken for ten seconds and then multiplied by six. The total represents the pulse beats per minute.

The closer the pulse rate is to 186 the harder the wrestler is working. To determine exactly how hard, it is necessary to know the wrestler's resting heart rate. If, for example, his working pulse rate is 160 and his resting heart rate is 60, it is apparent that he is working at 80 percent of his maximum capacity.

As a rule, the wrestler's output can be controlled in keeping with the objectives of the workout. The following three methods of training are based upon the concept of percentage effort: the extent of exertion relative to maximum physiological capacity.

PROGRESSIVE TRAINING

Consists of wrestling at a pace that increases with each timed effort. The first few repeats are performed at a relatively low level of exertion, after which the intensity is increased with each succeeding effort. The time of each repeat is decreased while the effort is steadily increased.

Effort	Time	Repeat	Cumulative Time Wrestled
25%	4 min.	1	4 min.
50%	3 min.	1	7 min.
75%	2 min.	1	9 min.
100%	1 min.	1	10 min.

Since a rest period of 30 seconds to two minutes is allowed between repeats, the total time comes to ten minutes (wrestling) plus one and a half to six minutes for rest.

REGRESSIVE TRAINING

Entails wrestling each repeat at a slower speed than the one before. Consequently, less effort is required with each repetition.

Effort	Time	Repeat	Cumulative Time Wrestled
100%	1 min.	1	1 min.
75%	2 min.	1	3 min.
50%	3 min.	1	6 min.
25%	4 min.	1	10 min.

Repeats are interspersed with a 30-second to two-minute rest period.

ALTERNATIVE PROGRESSIVE–REGRESSIVE TRAINING

Alternates fast hard repeats with slower, easier ones. Compared to the other training methods, the number of repeated efforts are greater, but shorter in duration.

Effort	Time	Repeat	Cumulative Time Wrestled
100%	½ min.	1	½ min.
25%	2 min.	1	2½ min.
75%	1 min.	1	3½ min.
50%	1½ min.	1	5 min.
50%	1½ min.	1	6½ min.
75%	1 min.	1	7½ min.
25%	2 min.	1	9½ min.
100%	½ min.	1	10 min.

Each training method has five variables that can be manipulated in order to control the intensity of the workout:
1. Duration of the training method
2. Pace of each repeat
3. Number of repeats
4. Duration of the rest interval
5. Nature of the rest interval

Workouts can be intensified by increasing variables 1, 2, 3, decreasing variable 4, or alternating variable 5 so that a mild physical exertion such as walking or stretching exercises replaces the inactivity of the rest interval.

Coaches need not guess at the amount of effort that is being exerted in a given bout or in a practice session. Thanks to this new technique they can fairly accurately assess the degree of effort put forth, as well as the level of difficulty of almost any phase of a workout.

9
Newer Approach to Wrestling Instruction

THE POPULARITY OF WRESTLING HAS BEEN INCREASING RAPIDLY IN RECENT years. Throughout the nation vast numbers of high schools, colleges, and universities have integrated it into their physical education and athletic programs. However, in spite of its rapid growth there are still many schools reluctant to include it in their curriculums. Their hesitancy, in many cases, results from the opinion that wrestling is a hazardous activity.

There is an abundance of available literature regarding safety in wrestling. A wealth of advice is provided on how the element of risk can be effectively reduced. Sound recommendations are offered in regards to improving instruction and/or improving facilities. Unfortunately, however, very little has been done to establish a programmed progression for teaching wrestling skills.

Every instructor and coach varies somewhat in his method of teaching. In wrestling, it's traditional to start by teaching those skills which could be employed from standing. It seems only natural that instruction should begin with standing techniques since regulation matches begin from a standing position.

The author would like to suggest a newer, better method of presenting wrestling skills divorced from this conventional approach. This newer method begins with wrestling instruction down on the mat instead of from standing.

The vast majority of injuries in wrestling occur during the early stages of instruction. Most of these are a direct result of falling and landing improperly. Falling from a standing position increases the chances of landing: (1) onto another participant, (2) off the edge of the mat, or (3) into an awkward position.

When falling to the mat (photo 31A) a wrestler commonly injures himself as a result of either poor physical condition or a tenseness

31A Falling to the Mat

which accompanies the fall. If he first learns to wrestle from a position on the mat, he has a better chance of becoming familiar with the activity before being taken down from standing.

Wrestling is a contact sport. Upon initial exposure to the activity, a novice is likely to be hesitant about falling. It is only after he gains confidence in his abilities that fears are gradually overcome and tenseness diminished.

As the foreign feeling that typically accompanies strange surroundings diminishes, the learner becomes more relaxed. Then, when he does fall, he is less likely to sustain an injury resulting from an arm or leg being too rigid as contact is made with the surface of the mat.

While down on the mat, the participant is developing a minimal level of physical fitness thus making it less likely that he will be injured later when he might fall incorrectly.

The ultimate in wrestling is to pin an opponent. The primary interest of the novice is to win. By initially being introduced to pinning combinations, an immediate understanding of how to defeat an opponent is realized.

Greater emphasis on safer teaching sequences can eliminate a number of injuries. Arbitrarily arranged or randomly chosen progression in skills learning has no place in education. The improper sequence can be hazardous. Good teaching requires adherence to better methods of teaching. Safer programs can never be achieved through complacency.

Research, to date, has been inadequate regarding methods for teaching wrestling. The lack of facts regarding the superiority of any particular method is disturbing. The absence of conclusive statistical evidence makes one opinion as correct as any other.

The existing studies on wrestling injuries makes it apparent that the vast majority take place during the first few minutes of practice or competition. The conclusion is generally that failure to warm up properly is the primary cause of these injuries. However, the fact that the first stage of a wrestling match is conducted in a standing position is commonly ignored. It is quite possible that the high incidence of injuries in the first few minutes is, in part, largely a result of the participants working from a standing posture. The remainder of the match is generally conducted in close proximity to the surface of the mat.

Attention is continually being directed toward newer teaching methods. Conscientious educators with an interest in upgrading instruction are constantly seeking newer ways of attaining more positive results. The physical education and coaching professions should be no exceptions. They, too, must be alert to newer approaches to teaching.

It is hoped that the information in this book will contribute to safer wrestling programs. If greater precautions are taken in setting up progressions, much can be achieved in minimizing injuries. While the possibility of eliminating all injuries can never be completely realized, the probability of their occurrence can be reduced.

The early phases of any wrestling program should be devoted to working on the mat instead of on the feet. Ground wrestling, either from a prone, supine, kneeling or referee's position should precede instruction from standing. Injuries can be reduced by having the participants wrestle close to the surface of the mat until a familiarity with the surroundings is realized. In this way, awkwardness is diminished and a moderate degree of fitness is developed. Wrestling on the feet should be delayed until at least a rudimentary knowledge of the activity is acquired and a minimal level of fitness realized.

Part III
TRAINING PHYSIOLOGY

10
The Science of Training

THE PRIMARY PURPOSE OF ANY TRAINING PROGRAM IS TO PREPARE THE athlete to perform at top efficiency while experiencing the least amount of fatigue. This purpose can only be realized through the application of the principle of adaptation.

Adaptation is the remarkable ability of the body to alter itself according to demands imposed upon it. The body will, in other words, strengthen itself as a means of better coping with requirements made upon it.

Adaptation is the basis for all training. It is founded upon the idea that the work capacity of the body increases as a result of having progressively greater demands imposed upon it. As the demands become greater, the level of physical fitness gradually improves to a point where work of a similar nature, amount, and intensity, when imposed, can be performed with less effort.

Once having adapted, the body can be made to adapt further if one increases the amount and intensity of the imposed demands. When these demands require the body to do work beyond that which can be performed easily, it will become further conditioned. The demands must be over and above previous requirements. As the demands increase, the body's ability to do harder work increases.

In order to gain results from any training program, the demands made upon the body must be sufficient to bring about adaptation. Adaptation can only be realized when the imposed demands are geared to levels above and beyond those which can be met comfortably. This progressive imposing of greater and greater demands is known as overloading.

Regardless of the type of method of training employed, there are six basic means by which the body can be overloaded: (1) by gradually increasing the intensity (pace), (2) by gradually increasing the duration of the work (time), (3) by progressively increasing the number of performances (repetitions), (4) by decreasing the time for recovery (rest), (5) by increasing the work effort during recovery (mild exercise), or (6) by any combination of the above five.

Training improves the body's endurance or, in other words, its ability to sustain or repeat prolonged activity in three ways:

1. By increasing movement efficiency and thereby reducing the expenditure of energy required to perform a skill. The more proficient an athlete becomes the less energy he needs to perform the skill.
2. By increasing the rate at which oxygen can be absorbed by the blood and transported to the muscles. This reduces the onset of fatigue.
3. By developing the ability to ignore the discomforts associated with fatigue. Willingness to accept pain complements efforts to sustain prolonged activity.

All three means of improving endurance require that the intensity of the work being performed reach a minimal threshold level. The heart rate, for example, must be raised to a value of 70 percent of the range that exists between its resting level and its maximal capacity, if improvement in endurance is to be realized. If the intensity of the work falls below this threshold level, no positive effects can be realized.

During the process of attaining and surpassing the minimal threshold level, the body experiences various responses. Hans Selye, author of *Stress of Life*—one of the most valuable pieces of literature ever written for coaching—has described the types of bodily responses made to imposed demands. These responses are as follows:

1. An initial response known as an alarm reaction characterized by increases in the (a) heart rate, (b) secretion of adrenaline, and (c) concentration of sugar in the blood is experienced by the body. This is the body's way of preparing itself for action. It is a mobilization of its resources. The blood flow is shifted from the viscera and skin to the muscles, the heart, and the brain. Adrenaline is shot into the bloodstream to strengthen the beat of the heart.
2. The second type of response entails more lasting adaptations. There is a decrease in the resting heart rate which suggests an improved capacity of the heart to pump greater amounts of blood with each stroke. This provides the muscles with larger amounts of oxygen and food substance while promptly removing lactic acid and carbon dioxide waste products. The venous return to the heart is greater and the volume of blood ejected with each beat is increased. This allows the heart a longer period of relaxa-

tion thus requiring less energy to perform a given amount of work. Also, the oxygen and carbon dioxide exchange in the respiratory system becomes more efficient.

3. The third response is detrimental. It results from too long an exposure to imposed demands. When this occurs, the adaptative capacity of the body is depleted. It is characterized by weariness, lack of energy, disinterest, loss of ambition, and a decreased morale.

James Councilman in his book *The Science of Swimming* makes a direct application of Selye's concept to athletic training. He suggests that an athlete training too little fails to attain maximum fitness while one who trains too hard experiences what is known as failing adaptation. He states that by relating the intensity and duration of imposed demands to the athlete's willingness to endure pain, the optimal type of response can be realized. The following chart taken from Councilman's book illustrates the idea of maximal adaptation.

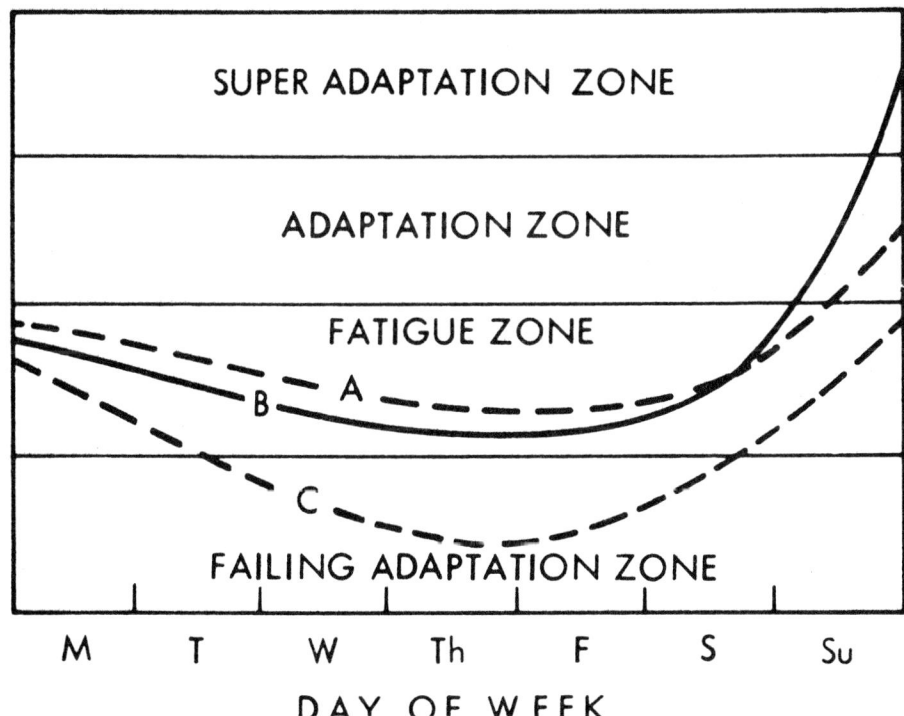

James E. Counsilman, THE SCIENCE OF SWIMMING © 1968. Reprinted by permission of Prentice-Hall, Inc., Englewood Cliffs, New Jersey.

The chart shows maximum adaptation being attained by athlete "B" who was willing to push himself close to but not into the failing adaptation zone. Athlete "A" was too interested in comfort to push himself far enough to make much of an adaptation. Athlete "C" pushed himself too hard. Maintaining an optimal work load while in the fatigue zone yields the greatest returns.

Conditioning is best realized in the fatigue zone. It cannot, however, be accomplished comfortably. It requires willingness to punish oneself to the point of acute discomfort.

Man has a natural reluctance to push himself to a point of discomfort. The burning lungs accompanied by anguished laboring for breath, a rapid pulse, muscular pain, and over all fatigue are difficult to accept willingly. Consequently, a mental block or barrier is commonly established. As the athlete pushes himself, this barrier is forced back further and further in bringing him closer to his physiological limit.

The athlete's psychological limit, however, is always reached before his physiological limit. Factors, such as motivation and willingness to accept pain, are primarily responsible for setting these psychological limits. Extensive research on these limits has been conducted by the late Arthur Steinhaus.

An athlete's physiological capacity is never truly known. However, as psychological inhibitions are removed the physiological limit is approached. Removal of these inhibitory influences occurs as the limits of tolerance to pain are extended. The physiological capacity of an athlete depends largely upon the degree to which he is willing to endure discomfort. Consequently, individual differences in the rate of adaptation may be explained partially upon the basis of the degree to which the athlete has been willing to punish himself. Willingness to accept pain is commonly the determining factor responsible for defeating a stronger opponent.

In conclusion, it must be remembered that conditioning requires that the body adapt to imposed demands. The body's capacity can only be improved by progressively imposing greater and greater demands. The effort required to do the same amount of work is less as the body adapts. Further adaptation is dependent upon increasing the amount and intensity of the work. Greater demands in the form of increased work loads must be imposed in order to bring about further improvements.

Demands imposed upon the body must be great enough so that a threshold level of adaptation is realized. This level should be sought by either increasing the pace or work load, or reducing the time of recovery.

The primary goal of overloading the body is the development of endurance. Endurance is improved by reducing energy expenditure, postponing the onset of fatigue, and increasing tolerance to pain.

The optimal level of exertion is the point just prior to entering the zone of failing adaptation. In order to attain this, the athlete must be willing to accept pain as a means of overcoming psychological barriers which might otherwise limit his physiological performance.

11
Interval-Circuit Wrestling*

COACHES WHO CANNOT FIND ENOUGH TIME FOR BOTH CONDITIONING AND skill teaching might find the answer in interval-circuit wrestling. This is a new and unique conditioning system that combines the principles of both interval and circuit training.

Interval training consists of repeated bouts of exercise interspersed with recovery periods of little or no activity. As the athlete's condition improves, the speed and length of each activity period is increased while the rest intervals are shortened.

Circuit training involves a series of activity stations at which one or more exercises are performed. The athlete moves from station to station until he completes the circuit.

Wrestling conditioning generally entails a combination of exercises and calisthenics. I believe this is a waste of time. Calisthenics seldom develop muscles in the manner needed for wrestling and they are usually so boring that the athletes find them difficult to perform with enthusiasm. Conditioning becomes drudgery and eventually kills morale. Workouts are dreaded, the season grows endless, and wrestling becomes unpleasant and unrewarding.

Interval-circuit wrestling eliminates this by adding variety to conditioning while helping the wrestler perfect his skills.

ARRANGEMENT OF THE INTERVAL-CIRCUIT

Frank Kapral's *Coach's Illustrated Guide to Championship Wrestling* provides the basic setup, as shown in the accompanying diagram. Using chalk or adhesive tape, we mark nine circles corresponding to the weight classes, each eleven feet in diameter and equidistant from one another on the mat.

---

* This article reprinted with the permission of *Scholastic Coach*, April 1971.

87 / INTERVAL-CIRCUIT WRESTLING

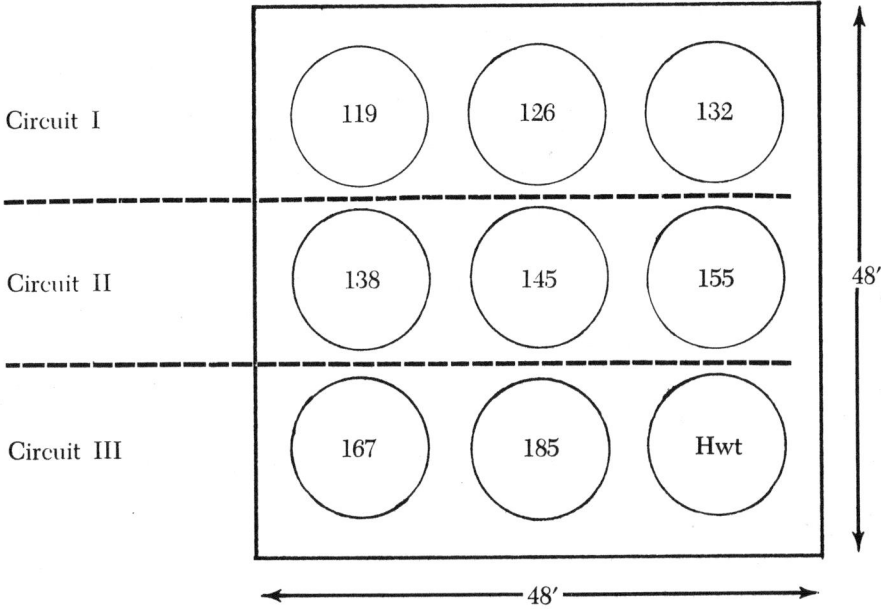

Each horizontal column of three circles constitutes a circuit, giving us a total of three circuits. Three wrestlers of approximately equal weight are assigned to each circle and given numbers from one to three.

The organization of the circuit system is delineated in the accompanying chart.

Round 1

Period	Resting	Wrestling		Position
1	1	2–3		Standing
2	2	1 (up)	−3 (down)	Referee's
3	3	1 (down)	−2 (up)	Referee's

Round 2

Period	Resting	Wrestling		Position
1	1	2 (up)	−3 (down)	Referee's
2	2	1–3		Standing
3	3	1 (up)	−2 (down)	Referee's

Round 3

Period	Resting	Wrestling		Position
1	1	2 (down)	−3 (up)	Referee's
2	2	1 (down)	−3 (up)	Referee's
3	3	1–2		Standing

In the first period of Round 1, wrestler number one rests while two and three wrestle from the standing position. After each takedown, they resume the standing position and try for another takedown.

In the second period of Round 1, two rests while one and three wrestle from the referee's position with one on top. If three reverses or escapes, they quickly resume the original position and begin to wrestle again when the bottom man slaps the mat.

In the third period of Round 1, three rests while two (on top) and one (on bottom) wrestle from the referee's position.

This continues through the next two rounds (see chart) for a total of nine periods. At the end of the first three-round series, a whistle or vocal command tells the number one man to move up one circle within the horizontal rows. Number one in the 119 circle moves to the 126 circle, number one at 126 moves up to 132, and the number one man at 132 moves to 119. The same rotation is followed in the other two circuits.

To facilitate the rotation, clear-cut instructions for the movement must be given in advance. After the first few times, the pattern will be thoroughly understood and should run smoothly.

After the second series of three rounds, the number two men rotate in the same fashion. This completes the interval circuit. Each boy has wrestled 18 complete three-period matches, 10 in his own weight class, against six different opponents. He has wrestled 18 periods standing, 18 periods in the top position and 18 periods in the down position. He has wrestled two-thirds of the time and rested for one-third.

Circuit I	119 Circle Wrestler	126 Circle Wrestler	132 Circle Wrestler
	1 — — — → 2 3	1 — — — → 2 3	1 — — — → 2 3
Circuit II	138 Circle Wrestler	145 Circle Wrestler	155 Circle Wrestler
	1 — — — → 2 3	1 — — — → 2 3	1 — — — → 2 3
Circuit III	167 Circle Wrestler	185 Circle Wrestler	Hwt Circle Wrestler
	1 — — — → 2 3	1 — — — → 2 3	1 — — — → 2 3

In organizing the interval-circuit, we suggest starting with 15-second periods and increasing to one minute as the season progresses.

ANALYSIS

There are five variables to the interval-circuit:
1. Length of circuit.
2. Intensity (speed or pace).
3. Number of circuits.
4. Length of rest.
5. Nature of recovery phase.

The degree of overload for the interval-circuit may be intensified by adjusting these variables as follows:
1. Increasing the time spent at each circle.
2. Increasing the pace of the circuit.
3. Increasing the number of circles.
4. Shortening the rest interval.
5. Increasing activity during the rest interval (jogging or mild exercise instead of complete rest).
6. Any combination of the above.

There are literally hundreds of combinations possible. The coach must decide which combination will produce peak performance in his situation. We recommend that the degree of overload of the circuit might be intensified most efficiently by:
1. Increasing the duration of each period to a maximum of one minute.
2. Shortening the rest intervals by using only two wrestlers at circles 126, 145 and 185. The rest intervals can be shortened further by having only two wrestlers at circles 119, 132, 138, 155, 167 and Hwt. while having three wrestlers at circles 126, 145, and 185.

LIMITATIONS OF THE INTERVAL-CIRCUIT

1. Fatigue interferes with skill mastery since the wrestler tends to substitute larger movement patterns for finer ones as he begins to tire. Preciseness can make the difference between the success or failure of a skill.
2. The circuit will do little to develop strength since the resistance (overload) cannot be scientifically controlled. It can, however, be regulated somewhat by requiring one of the wrestlers to react either passively, maximally, or with a certain percentage of resistance to his opponent's efforts.
3. The actual amount of work performed per unit of time (intensify) depends largely upon the pace at which the wrestler performs. He can push himself or take it easy. If the coach suspects that a wrestler is loafing, he should immediately check the boy's pulse to confirm this observation.

ADVANTAGES OF THE INTERVAL-CIRCUIT

1. Provides the physiological adjustments and the muscular and cardiovascular-respiratory endurance specifically required by the sport. (Actual wrestling is the best conditioner for wrestlers.)
2. Helps the wrestler master skills while conditioning himself.

In short, it is a simple yet practical means of achieving two goals simultaneously.

12
Strength Development for Wrestling

THERE IS NO SPORT IN WHICH THE PARTICIPANT CAN EMPLOY STRENGTH with greater effectiveness than wrestling. However, although it demands strength for success, wrestling does little to develop it to its optimal level. By itself, it is insufficient to develop the degree of strength necessary for top performance.

In the initial stages of conditioning, wrestling does to a limited extent strengthen the muscle groups involved, but as the level of skills improves, the actual amount of work done by the muscles is significantly reduced. Therefore, there comes a time when wrestling ceases to provide sufficient work to produce any appreciable gain in strength.

While there seems to be general agreement as to the relative importance of strength in wrestling, a difference of opinion exists as to which method is best for developing it.

Among the most popular means of developing strength are: (1) calisthenics, (2) isometrics, (3) metal springs, (4) rubber cables, and (5) weights. All impose demands upon the muscles. All require the muscles to do work beyond that which can be done comfortably. However, only through the use of weights can the overload principle be most beneficially employed in the development of specific muscles used in wrestling.

None of the other methods have the advantage of such a close degree of control. The use of weights provides a basis for controlling the intensity and duration of the resistance imposed with considerable accuracy. Progression can be observed and recorded. Moreover, weights can be adjusted to suit individual capacity.

Adjustable weights provide a basis for evaluating increases in strength while serving as a means of continuous motivation. By gradually increasing the weights being used, there is an assurance that the overload principle is being adhered to. In addition, any and all the muscles of the body specifically used in wrestling can be developed to their individual capacities. These factors, in combination, make weight training the most effective method of developing strength for wrestling.

Progress in the development of strength is evidenced in two ways. Increases in the amount of weight handled and increases in the number of repetitions a given amount of weight can be lifted (up to a point) are proof that strength is improving.

While the value of supplementing wrestling with weight training is becoming more and more recognized, the problem of selecting those exercises which will do the most to complement efforts to achieve strength still persists. The selection is difficult because of a lack of conclusive evidence regarding which muscles are primarily used in wrestling. Although research studies suggest the need for a certain amount of strength, there is no available literature which stringently identifies the major muscle groups used in executing wrestling techniques. Unfortunately, the failure to distinguish which muscles are most commonly employed in the sport has made it difficult to select exercises in planning conditioning programs. Since no study identifies the major muscle groups used in wrestling, selection is simply a matter of chance.

Each of the hundreds of skeletal muscles in the body has a specific action that is peculiar to itself. In planning a weight training program, it would be a mistake not to take into consideration those muscles that are used most commonly in wrestling. Any such program should emphasize developing strength in those muscles. A poorly planned program can be of little value. Exercises which do not contribute to those specific muscles should not be included. Only those which are particularly designed to strengthen the muscles associated with wrestling should be chosen.

There are many exercises that might be beneficial. However, only those which engage the muscles in a manner similar or identical to the actions of the wrestler should be selected. The importance of exercising these muscles in the same form they are used while wrestling cannot be overemphasized.

A coach leafing through much of the available literature will likely become confused by the wide variety of exercises suggested. His interest is primarily in those which will do the most to develop the strength required for wrestling success.

There is no shortage of opinions regarding which exercises are most beneficial. Authors disagree as to which exercises do the most to develop strength in wrestlers. While one emphasizes the importance of one set of exercises, another places his faith in a different, but often-

93 / STRENGTH DEVELOPMENT

times similar list. Perhaps it is this inconclusiveness that accounts for much of the confusion. Since no list of recommended exercises can be said to be completely accurate, none can be said to be completely wrong.

With this in mind, the writer conducted a survey of available textbook literature relating weight training exercises to the development of strength for wrestling. The purpose of the survey was to discover which exercises were most commonly selected by authors. A bivariate table was constructed as a means of pinpointing the most popularly listed exercises by authorities in the fields of weight training and wrestling. Among nine books surveyed, seven exercises were selected. These exercises are listed in the table below.

TABLE 2
Bivariable Chart Showing Frequency of
Exercises Selected by Authors

	Amer. Assoc. for HPER	Camaione & Tillman	Dratz, Johnson & McCann	Hoffman	Keith	Kapral	Murray & Karpovich	O'Shea	Rasch & Kroll
Rowing	X	X	X	X	X	X	X	X	X
Bench Press	X	X		X	X	X	X	X	X
Curls	X	X	X	X	X	X	X		X
Standing Press	X	X	X		X	X	X	X	X
Squats		X	X		X	X	X	X	X
Pull Overs	X		X	X		X	X		X
Sit Ups (weighted)		X			X		X	X	

EXPLANATION OF BIVARIABLE CHART

The purpose of the bivariate table was to determine which weight training exercises were most commonly recommended by authors of weight training and wrestling texts. Across the top of the table are the names of the authors of nine weight training and wrestling books. The left-hand column contains a list of the seven most frequently chosen weight training exercises for developing strength in wrestling. Any square on the table filled in with an "X" indicates the author listed above suggested the use of the exercise named in the left-hand column for developing strength in wrestling.

ANALYSIS AND INTERPRETATION OF DATA

Within the books surveyed, 35 types of exercises were listed for developing strength for wrestling. Seven of the 35 exercises appeared in four or more of the surveyed books. The analysis and interpretation of data is limited to these seven exercises.

The data in Table 2 show that rowing (standing and bent over) was the favorite exercise among the authors. The bench press, curls, and the standing press were the next most popular exercises.

The fifth most commonly mentioned exercise was squats (partial and full). Pull overs (straight and bent arm) and weighted sit-ups ranked sixth and seventh respectively.

Three of the top four exercises chosen (rowing, curls, and the standing press) are concerned with strengthening the arms. The body area that received the second most emphasis was the chest. Both the bench press and pull overs are directed toward developing this part of the anatomy. The final two areas of the body to which the authors focused their attention were the legs and the abdomen, in that order. Squats and weighted sit ups primarily concentrate on building up these areas.

CONCLUSIONS AND RECOMMENDATIONS

Muscular strength is perhaps the most important single factor in wrestling success. It can be built faster by coupling weight training with wrestling than by wrestling alone. In designing a weight training program, care must be taken so that exercises of dubious merit are not included.

Research has failed to advance supporting evidence for the inclusion or omission of various exercises for developing strength in wrestling. Since it is impossible at the present time to determine accurately which exercises are most beneficial, a survey was taken among leading figures in the fields of weight training and wrestling in order to get a consensus of opinion as a practical solution to this perplexing problem. Rowing, bench press, curls, standing press, squats, pull overs, and weighted sit ups were the most commonly mentioned exercises. They emphasize developing strength in the arms, chest, legs, and abdomen. It is recommended that any program of strength development for wrestling incorporate these exercises.

13
The Significance of Wrestling Endurance

ENDURANCE IS THE ABILITY TO ENGAGE IN REPETITIVE PROLONGED ACTIVITY without experiencing exhaustion or undue fatigue. In its broadest sense, it encompasses all the factors that enable a person to sustain performance to the point where fatigue sets in, thereby lessening efficiency or limiting further effort. It is primary dependent upon the efficiency of the cardiorespiratory systems.

Endurance is one of the most significant aspects of success in athletics. Many training programs and parts of programs are identified as enhancing endurance, and the possible benefits of participation in a sport such as wrestling are directly related to the effects of endurance training. Therefore, an important question is, "What is the significance of endurance?"

Participation in wrestling can result in the development of balance, agility, flexibility, strength, power, coordination, and endurance. Of these qualities, the last, endurance, is of primary importance.

The nature of endurance, particularly the physiological effect it has upon developing a more efficient functioning of the cardiovascular and respiratory systems, may be revealed by examination of its relationship to the expenditure of energy.

Practical application of the knowledge of how endurance relates to energy expenditure is based upon an understanding of the fundamental principle of intelligent and efficient conservation of energy as evidenced through the proper employment of body movement. It is only through such understanding that the relationship between various movements of the body while wrestling and the enhancing of endurance can be identified.

The importance of learning correct movement mechanics in the acquisition and perfection of wrestling skills as it relates to the physiological benefits of increased endurance often is unrecognized. In other words, the influence that skilled movement has upon improving the capacity for continuous exertion has frequently been overlooked.

There are two ways that a skillful movement can reduce energy expenditure and, thereby, contribute to improved endurance. The first is by efficient conservation of energy. This requires further explanation and amplification in order to be fully appreciated. For instance, the ability to move is fundamental to competition in all sports. But the ability to move effectively is quite different from just being able to move. This ability is developed through experience. It can be developed most readily when taught instead of being learned through trial and error. When correct patterns of movement are properly taught, movement is more physiologically economic, perfectly timed and correctly adjusted to produce the desired results.

While attempting to perform a new movement, many muscles that do more to hinder than enhance performance are likely to contract. By practicing the correct movement, useless and extravagant contractions are gradually eliminated and the pattern is done with greater ease and more efficiency. The more the correct movement is practiced the better it is learned. As proficiency in executing the pattern improves, the number of unnecessary muscular contractions becomes fewer. This results in a reduction in the amount of energy required to perform the movement.

In order to conserve energy, the level of performance must be high. Skillful performance results from efficient movement. It is characterized by an absence of unnecessary muscular contractions. The smaller the number of wasted contractions the greater the efficiency of movement. The more efficient the movement, the greater the amount of work that can be accomplished for the amount of energy expended. The more work that can be done the longer the performance can be continued. Thus, a harmonious cycle is established whereby endurance is prolonged to the degree the skill is perfected in performing a movement pattern. The greater the skill the less the energy expenditure resulting from the elimination of unnecessary movements. In the simplest terms, it amounts to doing the most with the least effort.

The second means by which an increase in the effectiveness of movement contributes to improved endurance is through the intellectual expenditure of energy. By intelligently expending energy it is possible to exhaust an opponent sooner.

The vast majority of wrestling matches are won on points rather than pins. Therefore, it stands to reason that the logical method of beating an opponent would be to wear him down. Wearing him down means decreasing his endurance or capacity for sustaining performance.

The two fundamental positions from which an opponent can be fatigued are: (1) on the bottom, and (2) on the top. If an opponent is made to work harder trying to escape than the man on top has to work to maintain control, he will expend more energy. He can be made to work harder if he has to carry the extra burden of the top man's weight. The longer he has to carry the weight while attempting to escape the sooner he will tire and the more likely it is that he will lose. By carrying most of the weight he also lightens the top man's load. The energy the top man saves will contribute to his endurance capacity and can be used later in the match, if necessary. The fact that the opponent has to expend more energy carrying his own weight plus part of the top man's, coupled with the idea that the top man has a lighter burden, will eventually result in his defeat.

While on top, it is most desirable to move on the feet, since this forces the opponent to constantly carry most of the weight. If the top man allows his knees to touch the mat, he lightens his opponent's burden and increases his own.

The second fundamental position from which energy can intelligently be conserved is on the bottom. To conserve energy intelligently, the bottom man should attempt to get to his feet as soon as possible. While down on all fours, energy is being wasted carrying an opponent's weight around. However, in a standing posture it is virtually impossible for the opponent to put his weight on the bottom man. As a result, he will have to carry the bulk of his own weight and will have no particular advantage. While standing, the bottom man will only carry his own weight.

In the referee's position, the wrestler on the bottom will tire sooner if he permits any part of his body, other than the soles of his feet, to touch the surface of the mat. By maintaining altitude he makes it very difficult for his opponent to put any weight on him. Therefore, he is less likely to tire as soon and is in the best position to force the opponent to carry the burden of his own body weight. Also, without the extra weight, he can move more efficiently and with less difficulty.

DRILLS ON MOVEMENT FUNDAMENTALS

The main objective of the following drills is to assist the wrestler in getting the "feel" of the positions that need to be assumed in order to do the most to enhance his endurance. These drills require that certain positions be assumed repeatedly in order to learn thoroughly and employ effectively the principle of energy expenditure. They are based on the idea that the wrestler should, whenever possible, move himself instead of his opponent.

SYSTEMATIC CHAMPIONSHIP WRESTLING / 98

Back Spinning Drill

This drill begins with one wrestler down in an all fours position with his head lowered. The top man places his chest, as a pivot point, on the back of the down wrestler. He spins around and around in quarter, half, and full turns making the bottom man bear his weight. He spins as rapidly as possible, and changes directions on the coach's command. He keeps his legs well back out of reach and uses them as seldom as possible for propelling his body around. He uses his hands to maintain balance, but never allows them to touch the mat.

A variation of this drill is to have the bottom man raise an arm to block the legs of the top man momentarily, if he fails to keep them out of reach.

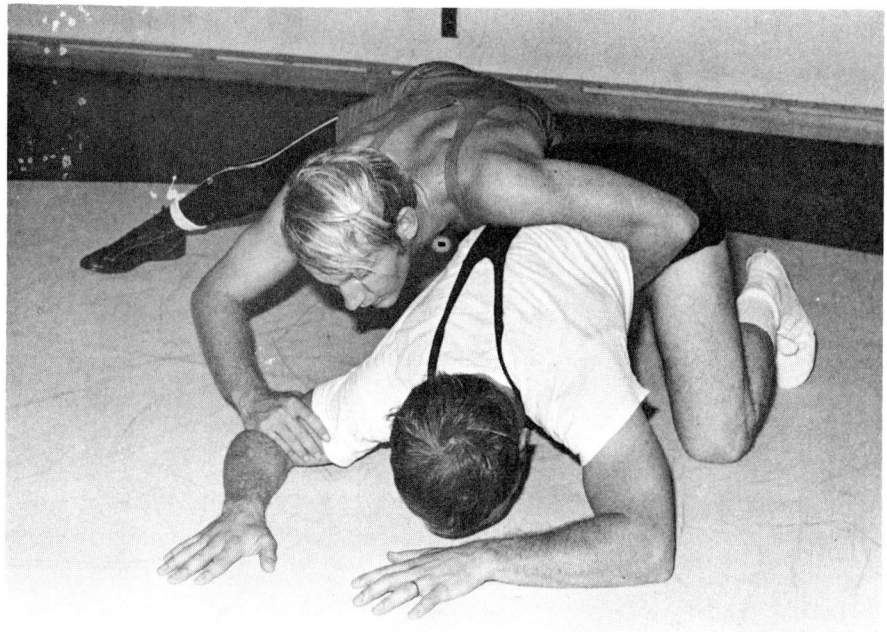

32A   Back Spinning

Floating Drill

The starting position of the wrestlers is the same as for the back spinning drill. This time, however, the bottom man is permitted to do anything to dislodge the man on top by the speed of his movements. Twisting, crawling, sitting out, and making circular turns are techniques commonly employed. He may not, however, stand up or use any grip, lock or wrestling hold.

The top man cannot use his hands to hold on, although he may use the inside of his arms to maintain a floating position. Almost all his weight should be over the bottom man and very little supported by his legs. He must move with the bottom man while attempting to keep his chest in contact at all times. This drill gives the top man practice in constantly being aware of the bottom man's movements and having to move with him in order to keep his weight on him.

33A Floating

Moving Up Drill

From the referee's position, the bottom man attempts to gain a standing posture, thereby removing the weight of the top man from his back. He is allowed to attempt anything that will enable him to secure a standing position. The top man must attempt to keep the defensive wrestler from gaining altitude.

Movement is used in executing every technique in wrestling. The need is for understanding the relationship between the skillful execution of that movement and the degree of expenditure of energy.

The more often a movement is practiced the more skillful the wrestler becomes. The more skillful he becomes the more improved his endurance becomes. The better his endurance becomes the greater are his chances of success. Through properly executed movements, desired success can be realized with the least strain and minimal expenditure of energy.

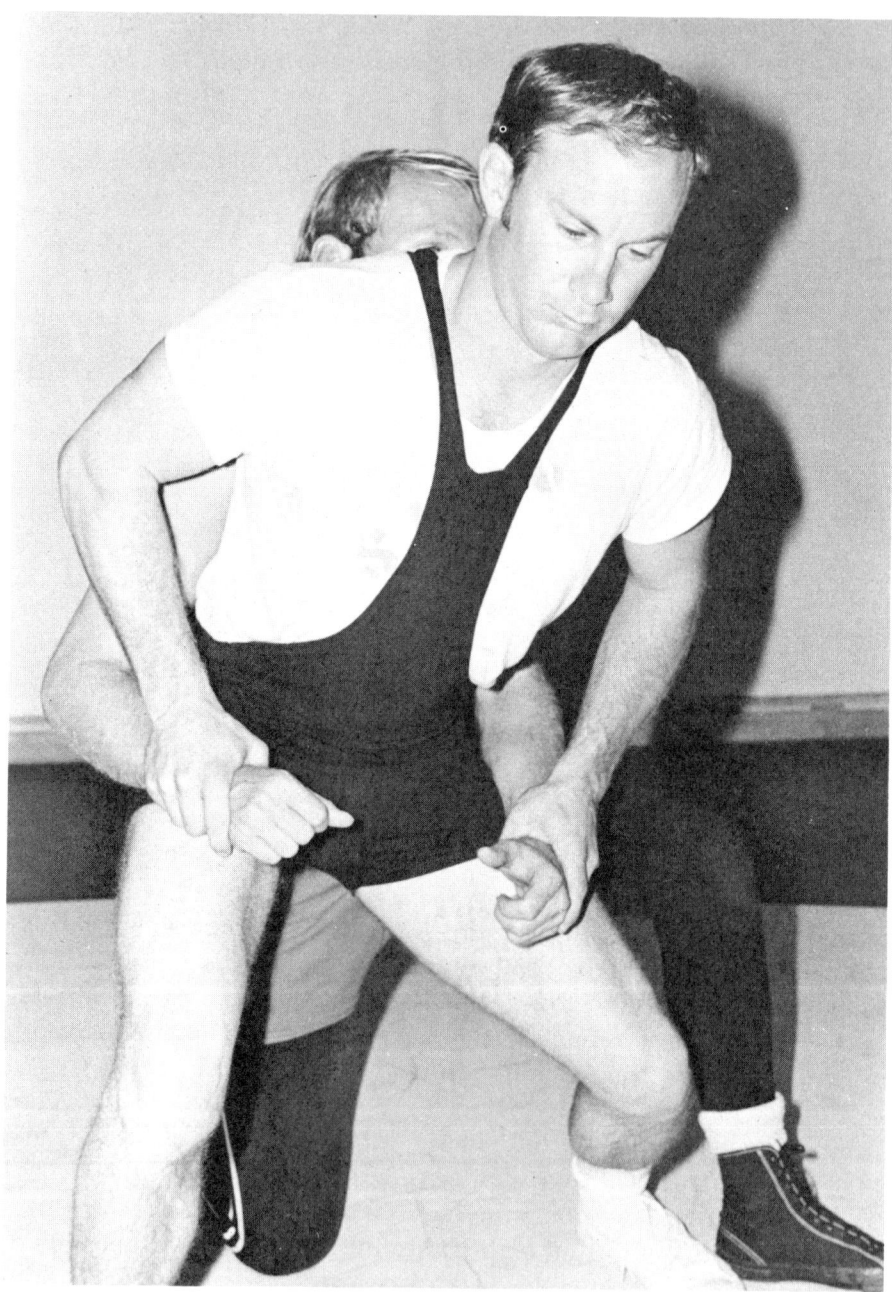

34A Moving Up

14
Fartlek Training in Wrestling

WRESTLING IS A SPORT THAT REQUIRES THE ATHLETE TO BE IN TOP-NOTCH physical condition. It is a sport where knowing all the holds in the world won't do the athlete a bit of good, if he can't compete for the full time of a regulation match without experiencing undue fatigue. It is a sport where being in condition means being able to pour it on in the third period and, if necessary, come from behind to win. It is a sport where more contests are lost in the final minutes because of poor physical conditioning than for any other single reason.

Diligent coaches are continually searching for newer, better methods of training. Most of the present methods do not vary greatly from one sport to the next. Wrestling, however, is an exception. It is, in many ways, notoriously antiquated in its concept of training.

The vast diversity of opinions regarding the relative merits of various training methods may be a principal factor in keeping wrestling from being introduced to some of the time proven methods used in many of its sister sports.

Coaches, skeptical of popular methods of conditioning athletes, tend to feel these methods fail to develop the specific type of endurance needed for wrestling. They are of the opinion that the best training for wrestling is wrestling itself. However, they fail to recognize the fact that these popular training methods can be adapted in such a way as to include actual wrestling as the prime activity.

Fartlek training is a well-established and extensively used method of conditioning athletes. It consists of exertion phases of relatively long periods of time at varying speeds. Its varying pace reduces boredom that commonly accompanies a more evenly paced training program.

In general, it is performed at a relatively slow speed and interspersed with an occasional hard and fast effort. The continuous uneven pace contributes to overall endurance, and conditions the athlete to perform at a faster tempo when necessary.

Fartlek training is generally emphasized in the early stages of conditioning although it is also used intermittently throughout the season. It can be employed as formally or as informally as desired. Three variations, ranging from the most formal to the most permissive, are presented below.

VARIATION #1

The first variation is a formal, rigid, and highly organized form of fartlek training.

PACE	TIME	CUMULATIVE WRESTLING TIME	WEEK IN SEASON
slow	5 min.	5 min.	1st
hard	3 min.	8 min.	
slow	5 min.	13 min.	
hard	1 min.	14 min.	
slow	5 min.	19 min.	
hard	3 min.	22 min.	
slow	5 min.	27 min.	
hard	1 min.	28 min.	
slow	5 min.	33 min.	2nd
hard	3 min.	36 min.	
slow	5 min.	41 min.	
hard	1 min.	42 min.	3rd
slow	5 min.	47 min.	
hard	3 min.	50 min.	
slow	5 min.	55 min.	4th
hard	1 min.	56 min.	
slow	5 min.	61 min.	

A slightly different version of the formal type of fartlek training session is known as the pyramid. As the name implies, it entails building up to a narrow peak from a broad base.

PACE	TIME	CUMULATIVE WRESTLING TIME	WEEK IN SEASON
slow	5 min.	5 min.	1st
hard	5 min.	10 min.	
slow	4 min.	14 min.	
hard	4 min.	18 min.	
slow	3 min.	21 min.	
hard	3 min.	24 min.	
slow	2 min.	26 min.	
hard	2 min.	28 min.	
slow	1 min.	29 min.	2nd
hard	1 min.	30 min.	
slow	2 min.	32 min.	
hard	2 min.	34 min.	
slow	3 min.	37 min.	
hard	3 min.	40 min.	
slow	4 min.	44 min.	3rd
hard	4 min.	48 min.	
slow	5 min.	53 min.	4th
hard	5 min.	58 min.	

VARIATION #2

A less formal form of fartlek training is to wrestle at a slow or moderate pace for approximately one hour, while increasing the pace only at times announced at the coach's discretion. Such announcements can be given as a verbal command or by a prearranged whistle.

VARIATION #3

The least formal and most permissive form of fartlek training is to permit the individual athlete to vary the wrestling pace according to his own discretion. In other words, each wrestler sets his own pace and varies it in accordance with how he feels at the moment. This is a very individualizing means of conditioning. It is commonly reserved for only the most dedicated and hard working athletes. It is quite popular with highly motivated individuals willing to push themselves beyond what is required by the more formalized variation. No direct supervision is provided. The only control is the amount of time this variation is practiced.

No one system of training is superior to another. No one single method will produce champions. No one particular method can develop all the qualities necessary to be a top contender. Only a combination of many methods will properly prepare an athlete for competition. The method emphasized at any one time should depend upon the goals being sought. It is only through the use of a variety of training methods that a wrestling program can be said to be complete. Fartlek training is only one of the methods that might be a part of that variety.

15
Marathon, Sprint, Interval, and Repetition Training Applied to Wrestling

WRESTLING—UNLIKE TRACK, SWIMMING, AND OTHER AREAS OF ATHLETICS—does not require the athlete to compete against a clock over a known distance. Consequently, many of the training methods popularly employed in other sports have not been applied to wrestling. It is the purpose of this chapter to apply, in a practical manner, some of these established training methods to wrestling.

Marathon training is called steady state training. It is mainly employed during the early stages of the season, but its occasional use throughout the year is not uncommon. It involves continuous activity at slow pace for an extended period of time. Its application requires wrestling at a slow pace for a time longer than that of a regulation match.

There are two primary advantages to this type of training. First, the athlete's confidence in being able to wrestle a match without experiencing undue fatigue is enhanced as a result of having trained for extended periods of time. Second, since the pace is much slower than that of an actual match he can concentrate more of his attention on perfecting techniques.

EXAMPLE "A" OF MARATHON TRAINING

PACE	TIME	SERIES OF REPEATS	REST INTERVAL	TOTAL TIME WRESTLED
slow	36 min.	1	0 min.	36 min.

EXAMPLE "B" OF MARATHON TRAINING

PACE	TIME	SERIES OF REPEATS	REST INTERVAL	TOTAL TIME WRESTLED
slow	9 min.	4	0 min.	36 min.

Sprint training receives emphasis late in the season. It is performed at a fast pace for the purpose of developing explosive speed. Because it involves all-out effort, it is very fatiguing and should be employed with discretion. Its indiscriminate use generally results in poorly and sluggishly executed skills.

The all-out wrestling efforts should be between one-half and one minute in length. They should never exceed three minutes. They may be conducted in an equal or an unequal series of repeats. The rest interval following each repeat should be long enough to allow the heart to return to approximately its normal level.

EXAMPLE "A" OF SPRINT TRAINING

PACE	TIME	REPEATS SERIES OF	INTERVAL REST	WRESTLED TOTAL TIME
all-out	15 sec.	6	1 min.	1½ min.

EXAMPLE "B" OF SPRINT TRAINING

PACE	TIME	SERIES OF REPEATS	REST INTERVAL	TOTAL TIME WRESTLED
all-out	45 sec.	1	3 min.	¾ min.
all-out	30 sec.	1	2 min.	1¼ min.
all-out	15 sec.	1	1 min.	1½ min.

Interval training involves repeated efforts interspersed with recovery periods of little or no activity. This provides for a frequent fatigue experience without the complete tiring effect of an all-out effort.

Interval training is a structured method of training requiring rigid controls. The pace, for example, should be equal to or faster than that of a regulation match. The time of each exertion should not be greater than one and one-half to three minutes. The rest interval should be long enough for the heart to recover partially. It should never be longer than the time of the repeated effort. This is rarely less than thirty seconds nor in excess of three minutes.

Pulse rate is the key to determining the times of the repeats and recovery periods. Many coaches have their athletes count their pulse. When it reaches 120 to 150 beats per minute the next bout is started.

EXAMPLE "A" OF INTERVAL TRAINING

PACE	TIME	SERIES OF REPEATS	REST INTERVAL	TOTAL TIME WRESTLED
moderate	30 sec.	30	½ to 1½ min.	15 min.

EXAMPLE "B" OF INTERVAL TRAINING

PACE	TIME	SERIES OF REPEATS	REST INTERVAL	TOTAL TIME WRESTLED
moderate	1½ min.	10	1½ to 3 min.	15 min.

Repetition training is a variation of interval training. It involves bouts of fairly long duration at a relatively fast pace and with sufficient rest intervals to allow for almost complete recovery.

Despite the fact that the pace is faster than that of a regulation match there should be no all-out efforts. Rather the wrestler should attempt to set a tempo he hopes to sustain when wrestling competitively.

The repeated efforts are often longer than those employed in interval training. They may range up to three quarters of the time of a regulation match, but never equal to or greater than that time.

The time for recovery should be at least three times greater than the time of each repeat. It is usually never less than one and one-half minutes. The pulse should be allowed to drop to between 100 and 110 beats per minute. Breathing should be permitted to return to normal and no discomfort should be experienced just prior to engaging in each repeated bout. Since fatigue will become more and more acute, the length of the rest interval should be increased as the training session progresses.

EXAMPLE "A" OF REPETITION TRAINING

PACE	TIME	SERIES OF REPEATS	REST INTERVAL	TOTAL TIME WRESTLED
faster than match speed	3 min.	8	9 to 12 min.	24 min.

EXAMPLE "B" OF REPETITION TRAINING

PACE	TIME	SERIES OF REPEATS	REST INTERVAL	TOTAL TIME WRESTLED
faster than match speed	4 min.	6	12 to 15 min.	24 min.

In each of the training methods discussed the factors of pace, time, series of repeats, rest interval, and total time wrestled were considered. The work intensity of each of the training methods can be increased by changing any of these variables in the following manner:

1. Increase the pace;
2. Increase the number of repeated efforts;
3. Increase the number of sets; e.g., wrestling for thirty seconds six times is considered one set;
4. Increase the number of times wrestled per day;
5. Increase the number of days per week wrestled;
6. Increase the altitude;
7. Increase the nature of the activity engaged in during the rest interval; e.g., mild exercise instead of lying down;
8. Increase the number of unfatigued opponents after each repeated effort;

9. Increase the number of unfatigued opponents after each set;
10. Decrease the amount of rest allowed after each repeated effort;
11. Decrease the amount of rest allowed after each set;
12. Decrease the time between daily workouts;
13. Decrease the time between days off per week;
14. Any combination of the above variables.

Since each variable can be controlled with a fair amount of accuracy, an evaluation of improvement and plateaus in conditioning is possible.

To be effective in improving the athlete's ability to perform with greater efficiency while experiencing less fatigue, these training methods have to be employed in a progressive manner. They should be initiated at a relatively low level and graded so as to increase the work intensity of each practice session. This will provide the necessary stimulus for maximal adaptation of the body.

No one method of training is superior to another in producing desirable physiological adaptations. None offers an all-inclusive answer. Each has its own advantages and limitations. Each is devised to condition the athlete in a slightly different manner.

The best approach is to include a variety of training methods into the program. Variety has the attraction of being able to reduce the chances that boredom and staleness will occur. The basis for emphasizing one method more than another at any one time during the season will be dependent upon the goals being sought.

Part IV
TAKEDOWNS

16
Coming to Grips

A PREREQUISITE TO TAKING AN OPPONENT TO THE MAT SUCCESSFULLY IS the acquisition of certain fundamentals. When there is insufficient opportunity to learn these fundamentals—the building blocks upon which success is dependent—difficulty is encountered in gaining takedowns. For example, when the fundamentals of tieing-up with an opponent fail to receive substantial treatment they are learned haphazardly. Negligence in emphasizing the correct manner of tieing-up decreases the chances of success in gaining takedowns. Too often tieing-up is taken for granted and too little attention is devoted to coaching its finer points. Sufficient time must be allowed for proper learning of this fundamental. Wrestlers not acquainted with how to come to grips with an opponent properly often feel that wrestling doesn't actually begin until after securing a tie-up position.

Any movement made with the intention of tieing-up should begin by walking in rather than reaching out for an opponent. Contact should first be made by catching one or both of the opponent's hands (photo 35A). This provides a certain amount of security in knowing, and in part controlling the location of his hands.

The grip on the hand should then be loosened in order to follow the surface of the opponent's arms upward toward the nape of his neck (photo 35B). Contact with the arm must be maintained all the way up to the neck. Once the back of the neck is reached it should be firmly grasped (photo 35C).

If the above procedure is adhered to religiously, it will prevent the opponent from capitalizing upon a mistake that might otherwise be made. The most common error made while tieing-up is that of reaching out for the nape of an opponent's neck. This mistake is an open invitation to be taken down.

There are many types of tie-up positions that can be assumed. One of the most common is the ear-to-ear and cheek-to-cheek (photos 36A and 36B). This tie-up position favors the stronger of the two wrestlers.

Despite its popularity, it is of limited value because very few takedown techniques can be employed from it. Unless a wrestler wishes to muscle his opponent or stall for time, this tie-up position should be avoided.

The inside double arm tie-up position is effective in keeping an opponent at a distance (photos 37A and 37B). Occasionally, an opponent's style will be dependent upon getting in close before going for a takedown. By positioning the arms inside the opponent's, he can be set up for an arm duck if he persists in his efforts to get close. If he reaches for a leg he can be dragged. If he hooks a hand under an armpit, he can be fireman carried.

A tie-up position that is commonly used to bait an opponent is the thumb trap (photos 38A and 38B). The thumb is placed on the inside of the opponent's elbow. The trap is baited by moving a leg out in front of the body so it appears as though it can be grabbed without much difficulty. When the opponent reaches for the extended leg the trap is sprung. The head is turned away while the opponent's elbow is lifted. Lifting the elbow is relatively simple since his momentum is already moving him in the desired direction. The maneuver is completed by going behind.

A less common but no less effective tie-up position is the monkey-on-a-stick (photo 39A). It, too, is good for setting up an opponent. A tremendous amount of leverage can be exerted once the opponent's arm is secured. By suddenly jerking down on the arm unexpectedly, the opponent is forced to bend forward. As he straightens, he sets himself up for an arm drag, duck, or fireman's carry.

The tie-up position most favored by the author appears in photo 40A. It requires keeping the head above the opponent's. A firm grip is carefully secured on the back of his neck. As long as the opponent's head is kept low, weight can be put on top of him. This tires him while lightening the wrestler's own burden.

The free arm should be used to keep the opponent from moving in too close. By maintaining some distance from the opponent, greater maneuverability is realized. Ability to remain mobile is one of the most important factors in securing takedowns. Being free to move around without difficulty is essential in setting up an opponent. If, while moving about a tie-up position is not to the wrestler's liking, he should back out and start again.

To be a successful competitor the mastery of fundamentals is a must. One of the most basic fundamentals is the ability to properly tie-up with an opponent. Proficiency in coming to grips safely must be taught early and continually practiced throughout the season. It should be a regular part of executing every takedown and reviewed on a periodic basis.

113 / COMING TO GRIPS

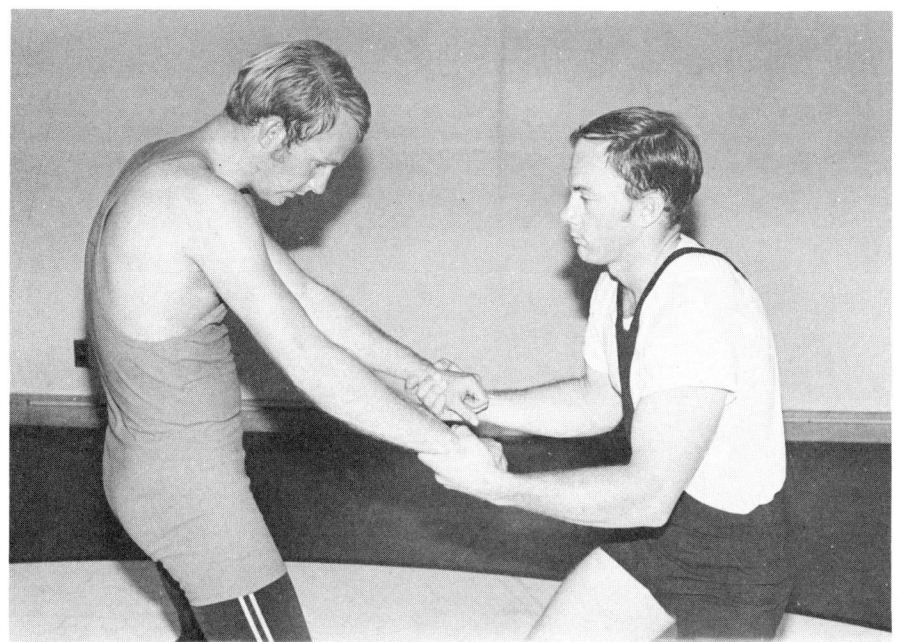

35A Tieing Up. Catching opponent's hand.

35B Maintaining contact with opponent's arm.

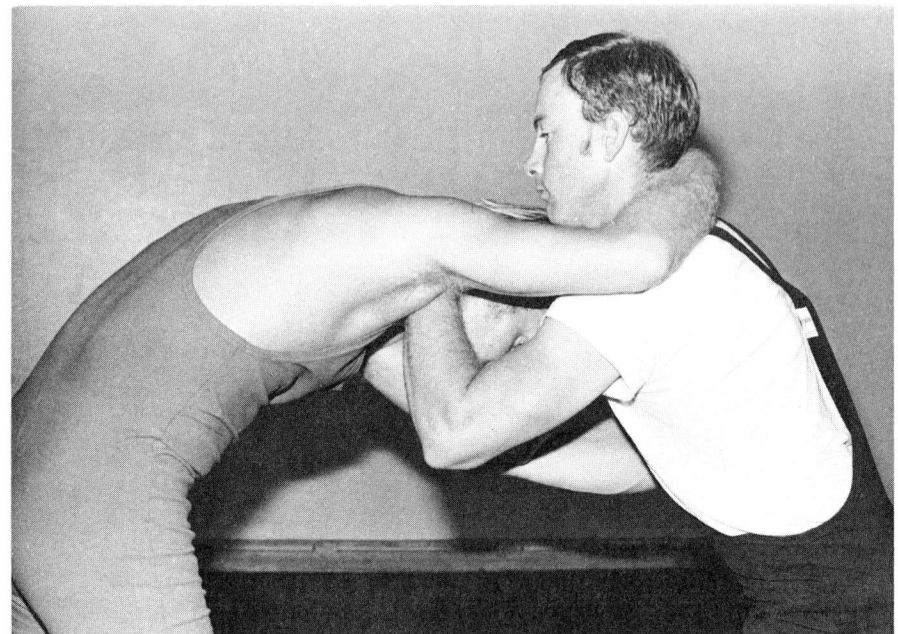

35C Grasping hold of opponent's neck.

36A Ear-to-Ear and Cheek-to-Cheek Tie-Up

115 / COMING TO GRIPS

36B   Ear-to-Ear and Cheek-to-Cheek Tie-Up (Bottom View)

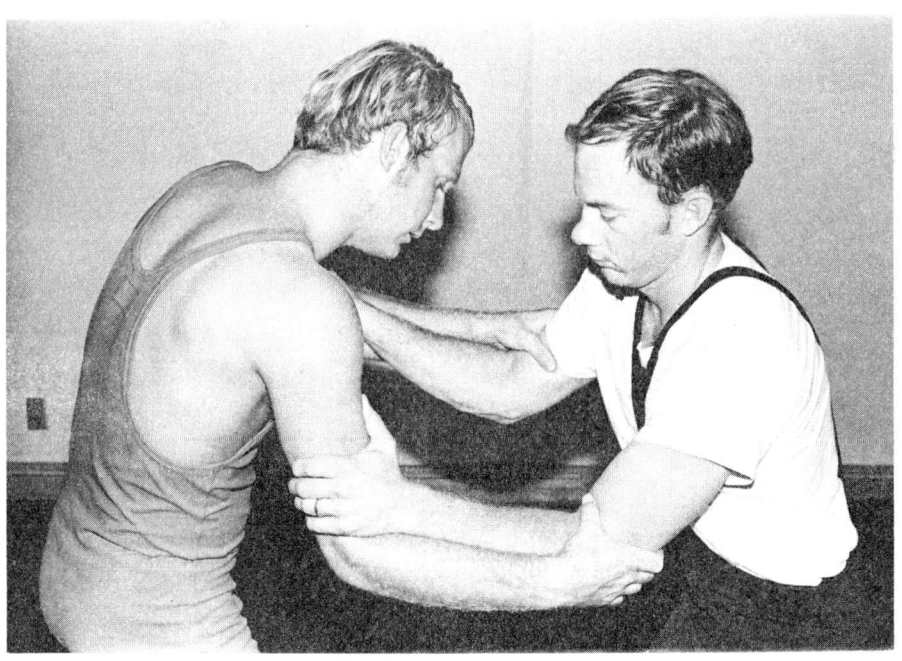

37A   Inside Double Arm Tie-Up

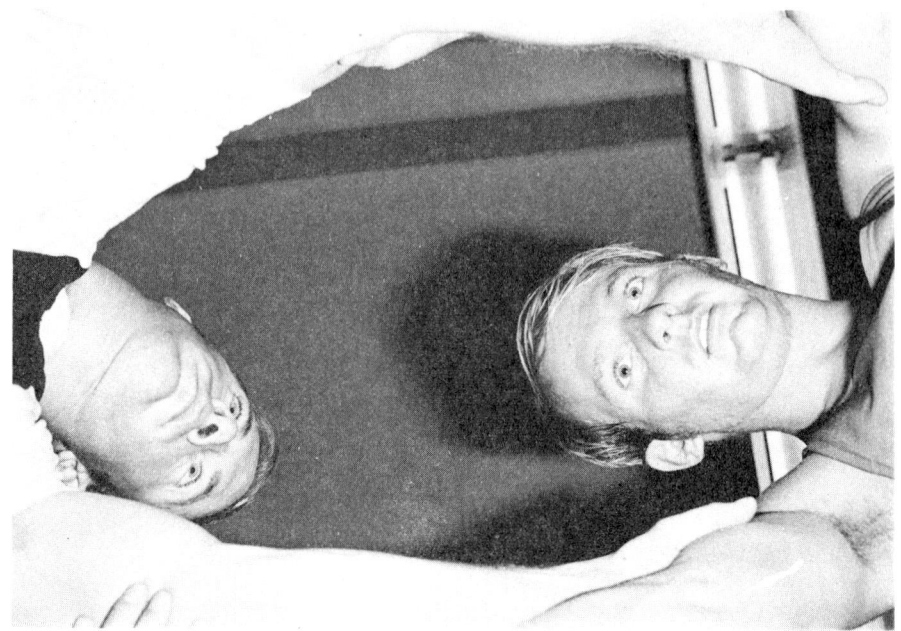

37B   Inside Double Arm Tie-Up (Bottom View)

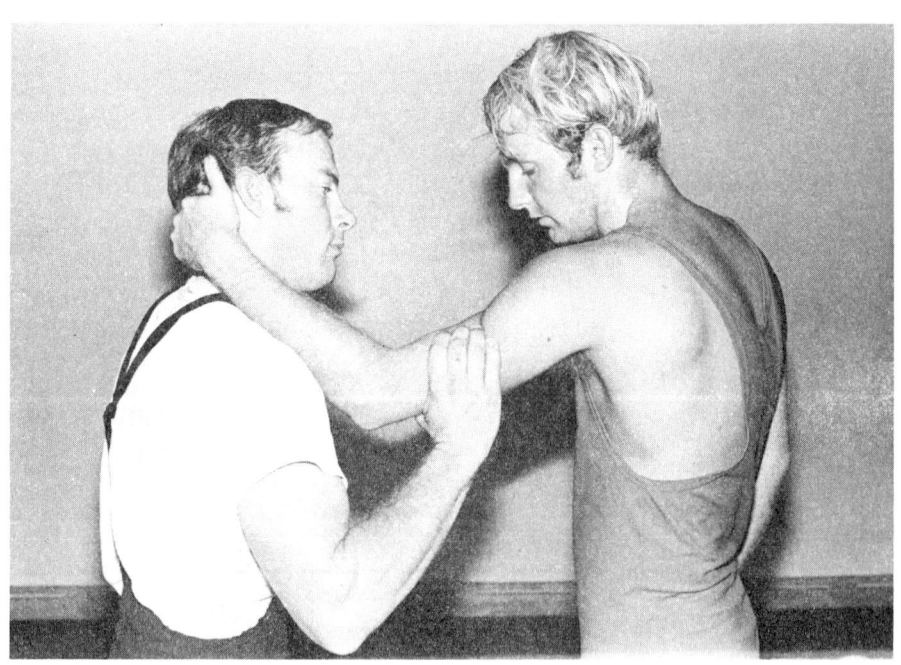

38A   Thumb Trap Tie-Up

117 / COMING TO GRIPS

38B Thumb Trap Tie-Up (Side View)

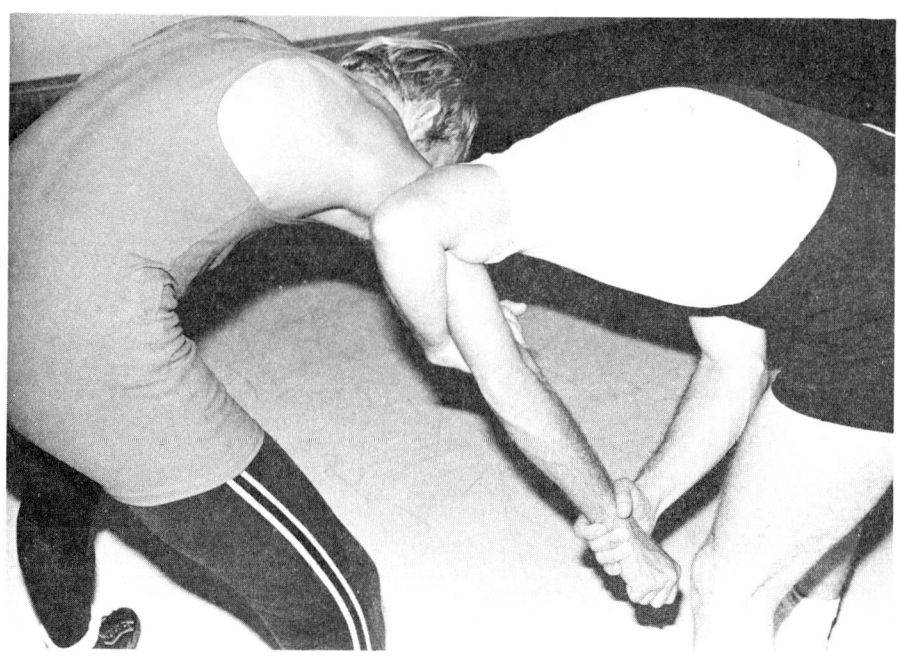

39A Monkey on a Stick Tie-Up

40A Favored Tie-Up

17
Major Weaknesses of Various Wrestling Stances

NOT ALL WRESTLING STANCES ARE EQUALLY EFFECTIVE. EACH HAS ITS own innate weaknesses. Knowing what these are can enhance the chances of success, because capitalizing upon a weakness offers a means of gaining a definite advantage.

There are almost as many stances as there are styles of wrestling. This chapter will be concerned with some of the more popular ones.

Flatbacking (photo 41A) is best described as a stance in which the wrestler's back is more or less parallel to the surface of the mat. It is

41A   Flatback Stance

most popular with novice wrestlers. It has the characteristic of offering a false sense of security. The inexperienced wrestler tends to feel he is least likely to be taken down when his legs are as far away from his opponent as possible. The greater the distance the safer he feels.

Flatbacking gives him more time to react defensively to any attempt to reach for his legs. While it is true that this stance does offer a certain degree of protection from leg takedowns, it also leaves the wrestler more vulnerable to other types.

The major weakness of the flatbacking stance is the lack of stability that results from a forward displacement of the wrestler's center of gravity. When the center of gravity is directly over the supporting base, the body is perfectly balanced.

Stability, or the capacity of the body to return to its original position, is reduced when the center of gravity falls outside the supporting base. Anytime the center of gravity is beyond the supporting base, the body is less stable. For example, if a limb is moved from its original location, another part of the body must be moved in the opposite direction in order to bring the center of gravity back over the base.

After being pushed or pulled, the flatbacker is required to make instantaneous adjustments in order to maintain balance. The time during which these adjustments are being made is when he is most vulnerable.

An effective technique for taking down a flatbacker who leans forward is the head snap, sometimes referred to as the snap down. If the flatbacker chooses to back away instead of lean forward, he can be taken down with an ankle pick-up.

Another popular stance is down on one knee (photo 42A). A wrestler who is on one knee is limited to essentially a leg drive attack. A leg drive is the only effective takedown technique his opponent has to defend against.

A leg drive can be effectively avoided by circling in the direction opposite to the knee that is on the mat. Moving away from the strength of his rear foot does a great deal to handicap his style. It keeps him from being able to set himself in preparation for executing a leg drive.

The fact that many wrestlers are not used to sparring with a man employing this type of stance puts them at a slight, but significant disadvantage. Anything foreign or unfamiliar will create a certain amount of uncertainty.

The wrestler in this stance is weakest in the direction of the knee that is on the mat. This is where he is least stable. This is where he is least able to cope with pressures in a sideward direction. By tieing up

121 / MAJOR WEAKNESSES OF VARIOUS STANCES

42A One Knee Stance

the hand that is on the same side of the body as the down knee, he becomes vulnerable to being tipped over onto his back. Force exerted in that direction makes it difficult for him to keep from falling over.

In addition to limiting the methods of attack, a one-knee stance also limits the wrestler's mobility. Forward and backward movement is difficult, while sideward movement is impossible.

Mobility is restricted almost entirely to rotation in a circular fashion. Any other movement must rely totally upon the explosive force of the rear foot. In order to create force the toes of this foot must be coiled so as to produce some tension against the surface of the mat.

For these reasons the author does not recommend the use of either the flatback or the one knee stance. Instead a more erect type of stance is suggested (photo 43A).

In order to best understand the basic reasons for assuming the more erect type of wrestling stance, specific aspects of the stance will be discussed in accordance with various segments of the anatomy.

For clarity, the parts of the body have been divided into three broad areas. The first area extends from the head to the shoulders. the head should be held high. If it is downward, vision will be impaired resulting in the wrestler being more vulnerable to being taken down.

The eyes should be focused mainly upon the opponent's midsection. Focusing attention upon other areas—such as an opponent's head, eyes, or legs—is likely to result in being fooled by fakes, feints, and distracting movements. It should be remembered that an opponent has to move in the direction of his waistline.

The second area of consideration is from the shoulders to the waist. The arms should be bent and the elbows kept in close to the body. One hand should be extended slightly ahead of the other, with the palms of both hands turned down. The movements of the hands should always be downward in direction to avoid a tie-up that might anchor the appendage to the opponent. Palms turned upward become defensive and useful only for catching and stopping an opponent's charge. This results in having to support his weight and leaves the wrestler open to be taken down with a fireman's carry or duck under.

The body should be bent forward slightly at the waist. The back should remain fairly straight. This puts the body in an erect posture, a bit forward, but never so far forward that it causes the wrestler to lean into his opponent.

The third area of the body is from the waist down. The knees

123 / MAJOR WEAKNESSES OF VARIOUS STANCES

43A   Erect Stance

should be bent so as to place the body in a slight crouch. This facilitates quick movement in any direction. If the knees were kept straight difficulty would be encountered in moving. The weight should be over the balls of the feet, thus allowing for greater agility. A flat footed wrestler is slow, early to tire, and easily upset.

The feet should be spread. Stability is directly proportional to the area of the body's supporting base. With the feet too close together stability is very poor and the wrestler is easily pushed or pulled off balance. The feet can be too wide as well as too close together. If the feet are spread too wide, it increases stability but reduces mobility. In general, mobility is more desirable than stability. Being free to move instantly in any direction is invaluable.

Stability can be enhanced by placing one foot slightly ahead of the other. While moving about the feet should never be crossed. Movement should result from sliding across the mat at short distances.

After weighing all the advantages and disadvantages of the various types of stances, the most superior in terms of mobility and potential effectiveness is the more erect type.

18
Upsetting an Opponent's Balance

THE FACT THAT THERE ARE TWO TYPES OF BALANCE, PHYSICAL AND mental, goes commonly unrecognized among those involved with wrestling. It is only after this duality is realized and accepted that setting up an opponent can be taught effectively.

Before physical balance can be destroyed, mental balance must first be attacked—a strategem best accomplished by employing the element of surprise. Any tactic which is unexpected and momentarily disrupts an opponent's train of thought can be employed. Anytime the opponent is forced to take time to adjust his thinking in order to comprehend and subsequently cope with a new set of circumstances, his mental equilibrium is unstable. At this precise moment, offensive action must be undertaken to destroy his physical balance. It is during the split second the opponent is adjusting his thoughts that he is most vulnerable.

Initiating a move that is momentarily distracting is an effective means of upsetting an opponent's mental balance. The distraction is executed with the intent of getting him to react in an anticipated manner. His expected reaction, if forthcoming, is then capitalized upon.

One popular method of distracting an opponent is to strike his forehead or shoulder (photos 44A and 45A). This will annoy and aggravate him. Just about the time he anticipates being struck again, shoot for his legs. Another common method of distraction is to have an opponent resist the pressure of a hand on the back of his neck. Then a sudden release of the pressure will cause him to unconsciously straighten up and thus expose his legs momentarily.

A good deceptive move is one that looks exactly like the start of a sound offensive maneuver. By leading an opponent to believe that some technique is about to be attempted, he will likely try to avoid the imagined danger and thereby unknowingly leave himself vulnerable to the application of the intended technique. Thus his efforts to avoid the imagined danger are utilized to his disadvantage.

SYSTEMATIC CHAMPIONSHIP WRESTLING / 126

44A Striking Opponent's Forehead

45A Striking Opponent's Shoulder

The essence of wrestling strategy is to get the opponent to move or exert force in a desired direction so as to jeopardize his equilibrium. An opponent who reacts in the manner he would have if the deceptive attack had been authentic is vulnerable. Offensive action must then be swiftly employed. A slight delay may make the difference between success and failure. Once an opponent's balance has been destroyed, he must be kept struggling to regain it.

A feint or fake is such a deceptive move, designed to lead an opponent to believe that an offensive attack is being initiated. To deceive an opponent successfully, the feint must look exactly like the beginning of an offensive attack. An example of an effective feint is illustrated in photos 46A through 46D. Here the defensive wrestler's main objective is to get the opponent to step away from the arm that is being moved toward his crotch. By moving away, the opponent exposes himself for a switch to the opposite side. The first move is a feint which places the opponent in position to be switched by a second genuine attempt. To further confuse the opponent, the first move can be initiated as a genuine attack. This makes it difficult for even the most experienced opponent to determine whether the first action is preliminary or primary.

An opponent who can detect when a particular move is going to be made is usually able to block or counter regardless of how effectively it may be executed. However, this ability to detect moves in advance can also be used against him. By intentionally telegraphing or giving advance notice of what is supposedly going to be attempted, the opponent can be enticed into moving to a vulnerable position. For example, the eyes can be used to convey the idea that a move is about to be made in a given direction. By focusing attention on a spot other than the direction truly intended, real intentions can be disguised and used to confuse the opponent. Consequently, when the intended move is made it is more likely to be successful since it will be totally unexpected.

By anticipating, it is possible to take advantage of an opponent's weakened position at the instant it occurs. Moves can thus be planned so as to place an opponent in a position that leaves him open to attack. Situations can purposely be created so as to correctly predict what an opponent will do.

If an opponent can be made to move in a set pattern, it is possible to predict where he will be positioned at any one moment. By planning movements so as to put an opponent in a particular position at a precise moment, success is almost assured. For example, by getting

46A Standing Switch. Faking the switch to one side causes the opponent to move in the opposite direction.

46B Grasping opponent's hand while reaching back to the inside of his leg.

SYSTEMATIC CHAMPIONSHIP WRESTLING / 130

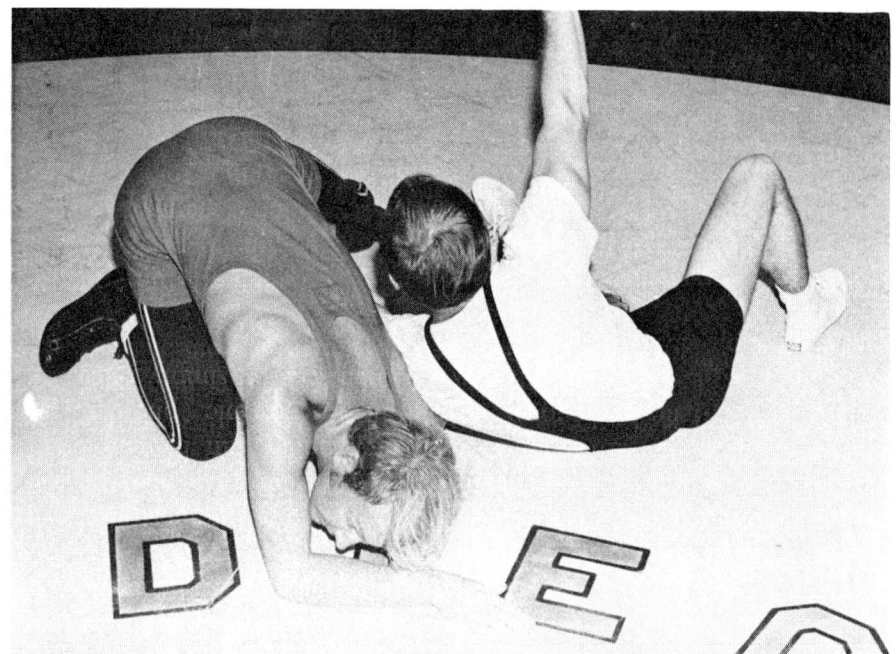

46C Sitting down.

46D Turning to a position on top.

131 / UPSETTING AN OPPONENT'S BALANCE

an opponent to move in a circular pattern it is possible to predict when his weight will be over one leg. It is relatively easy to capture that leg since it cannot be moved until the weight is transferred to the other leg (photo 47A).

Variations to techniques are vital ingredients for setting up an opponent. For example, if while initiating an arm duck the opponent reacts by pulling the arm down, the momentum of his reaction can be used to drag him (photos 48A and 48B). If he leaves it up, the arm duck can be completed (photo 48C). While, if in the process of ducking he pushes forward, a fireman's carry can be employed (photo 48D). Or, if he backs away, a single leg pick up is possible (photo 48E). It is always a good policy to arrange things so that anything the opponent does is wrong. There are many possible combinations. With a little imagination and experimentation, a phenomenal number can be worked out.

The double leg takedown (photo 49A), is one of the most effective set-ups for a variety of takedowns. If after securing a hold of the opponent's legs, he drives forward a duck under can be employed (photo 49B). If he backs away, a back heel is possible (photo 49C). If he sprawls, a single leg takedown is available by simply releasing one leg (photo 49D).

47A Single Leg Dive

48A Arm Duck. Lifting opponent's arm prior to ducking under.

133 / UPSETTING AN OPPONENT'S BALANCE

48B   Reacting with an arm drag after opponent pulls arm down.

48C Slipping head under opponent's raised arm when he leaves it elevated.

135 / UPSETTING AN OPPONENT'S BALANCE

48D Employing a fireman's carry when opponent drives forward.

48E Securing a single leg pick-up when opponent backs away.

137 / UPSETTING AN OPPONENT'S BALANCE

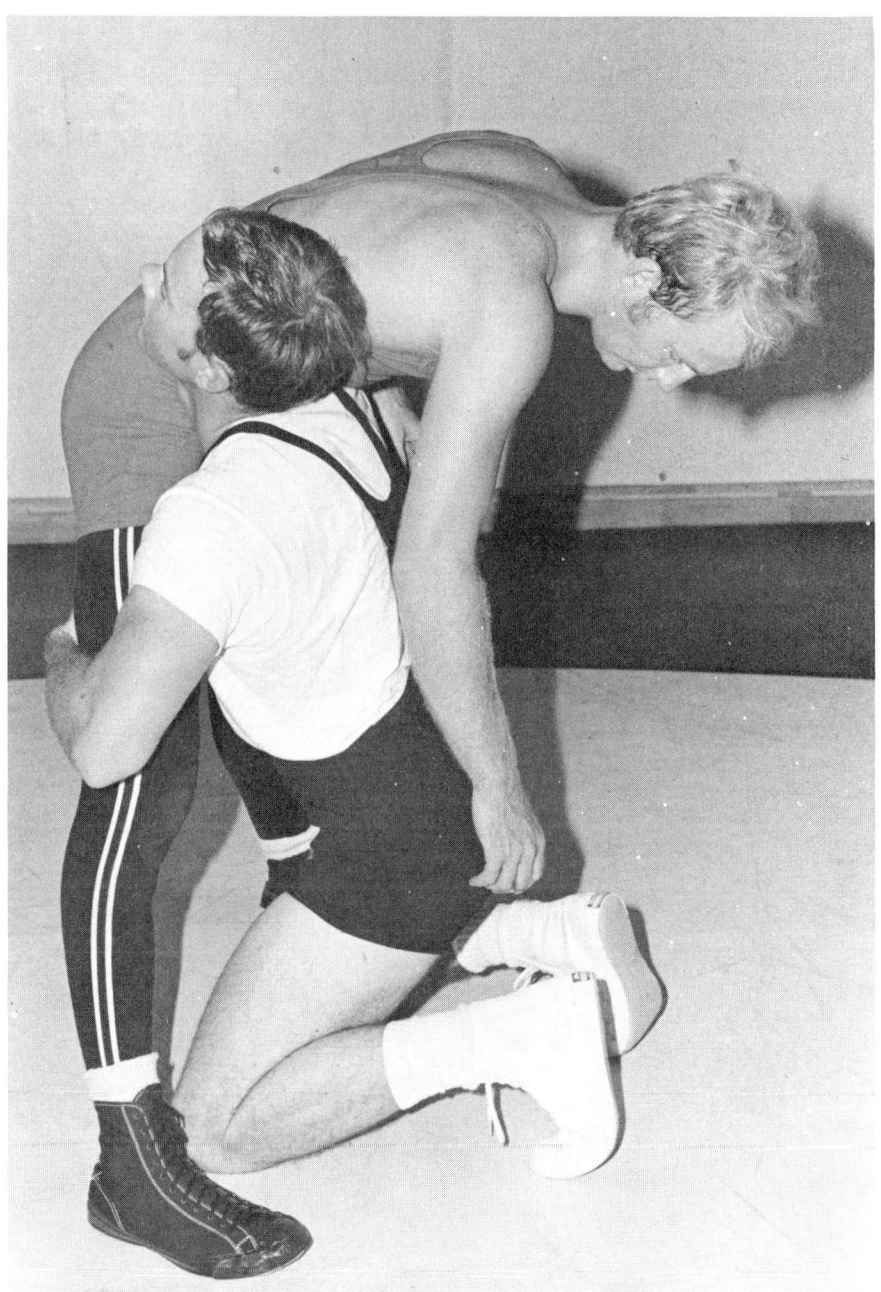

49A Double Leg Dive. Dropping to both knees while securing a hold of opponent's legs.

49B Ducking under opponent's arm if he drives forward.

139 / UPSETTING AN OPPONENT'S BALANCE

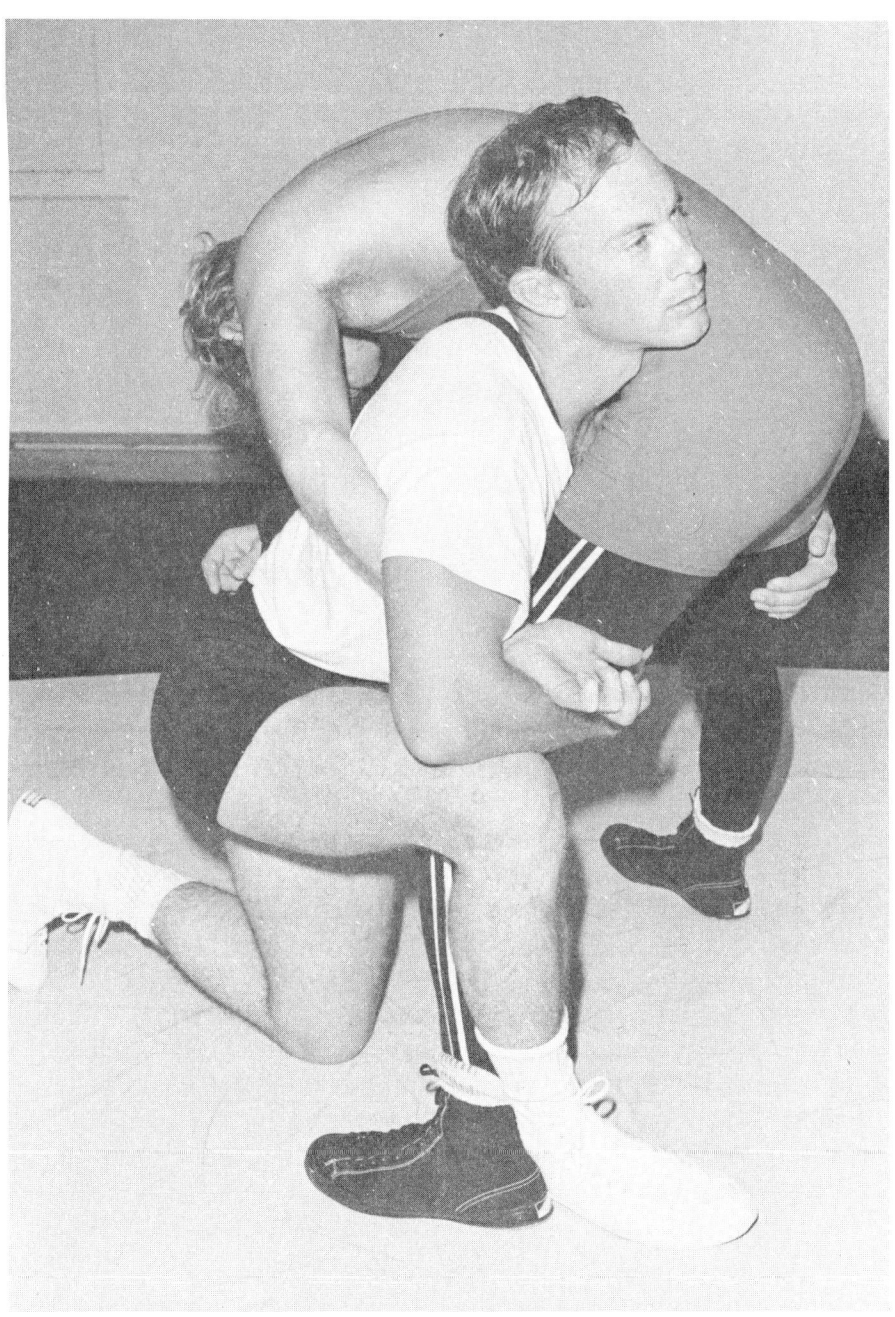

49C Employing a back heel if opponent backs away.

49D   Gaining a single leg takedown if opponent sprawls.

Less total effort has to be exerted in getting an opponent to move in a desired direction by encouraging him to resist a force in the opposite direction than by pushing or pulling him in the favored direction. It is better to jolt an opponent than it is to push or pull him.

Jolting has no follow through. It is a crisp force executed only with the strength of the arms. There is no shifting of the body's weight. After jolting, an opponent's reaction should be capitalized upon.

An opponent who assumes a stance with his upper body parallel to the mat should be jolted downward. When he resists the jolt, he sets himself up for a head snap (photos 50A and 50B). If he does not resist, he can be encouraged to do so by extending constant pressure on the back of his neck while taking short, quick steps backward in a wide arcing pattern. In order to maintain his balance, he must move forward, thus setting himself up for the head snap. If he attempts to back away, he can be taken down with an ankle pick up (photos 50C and 50D).

Techniques are only as good as the moves used to set them up. They should never be attempted until the opponent is off-guard or in a position to be "taken." Too often techniques are attempted with no preliminary movement. A set-up must be made so as to place the opponent in a weakened position if he is to be taken down, controlled, or pinned.

141 / UPSETTING AN OPPONENT'S BALANCE

50A Head Snap. Staying above opponent and placing pressure on the nape of his neck.

50B Snapping opponent's head downward if he resists the pressure.

50C Grasping opponent's leg if he backs away while maintaining pressure on the back of his neck.

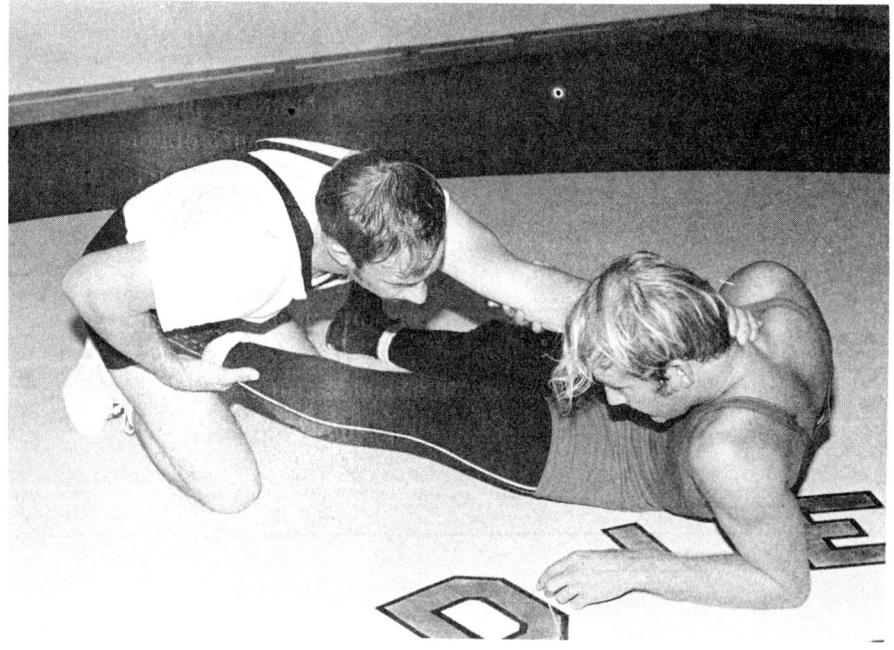

50D Controlling opponent on the way down to the mat.

19
Baiting an Opponent

MOST OF THE CURRENT WRESTLING LITERATURE AMPLY DESCRIBES THE sequence of moves required to perform the various illustrated techniques properly. However, essential preliminary moves necessary to prepare an opponent for the moment of successful execution of these techniques are generally missing.

Fundamental to the successful execution of any wrestling technique is the set up. This requires initiating specific moves for the purpose of getting an opponent to react in a predicted manner.

In most cases, an opponent can be expected to attempt to capitalize upon a move that he perceives as a mistake. Moves perceived as mistakes or weaknesses are useful in "baiting" an unwary opponent.

Baiting is a clever means of tempting, enticing, or luring an opponent into making a move that will weaken his position. In most instances, it requires exposing part of the body as an invitation for the opponent to attempt some obvious technique. From all outward appearances it would seem to the opponent that an excellent opportunity exists for employing such a technique. Thus, he is drawn off-guard to an attractive opening for which a counter has been prepared. When he attempts to take advantage of this opportunity the counter is applied. The discovery that he has been tricked is only realized after it is too late.

A prime example of a baiting type of set up is illustrated in photos 51A through 51C. While in a fairly erect standing neutral tie-up position, move the palm of the hand to a position under the opponent's elbow. It is important that the thumb be situated on the inside of the opponent's elbow (photo 51A).

The leg, as bait, is placed out in front of the body so as to appear as though it can be grabbed without much difficulty. When the opponent reaches for the extended leg, simply lift up on his elbow (photo 51B). Lifting is relatively easy since his momentum is already moving him in that direction. Complete the maneuver by going behind (photo 51C).

SYSTEMATIC CHAMPIONSHIP WRESTLING / 144

51A Thumb Trap. Tieing-up with a thumb under opponent's elbow.

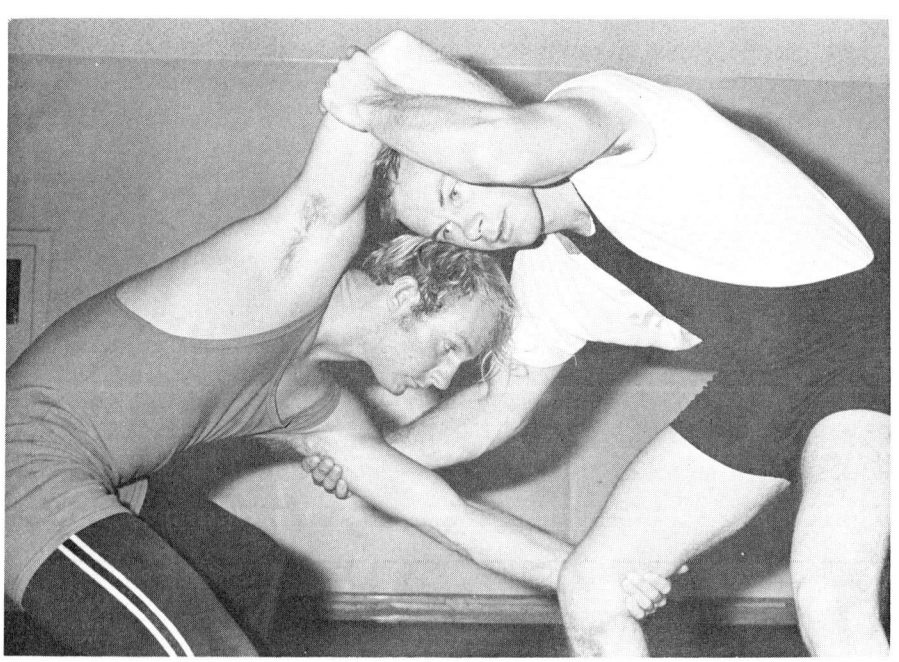

51B Pushing up on opponent's elbow as he reaches for a leg.

145 / BAITING AN OPPONENT

51C Stepping forward and to a position of control.

Setting up an opponent is not confined to takedown situations. In addition to baiting for a takedown, an opponent can also be baited into a pinning situation.

In the riding position shown in photo 52A, the leg is again used as bait to entice an opponent into making a mistake. By bringing the leg within the reach of the opponent, he is tempted to grab for it. As he does, he places himself in a very precarious position (photo 52B). By bringing an arm down onto his neck he can be forced onto his back (photo 52C).

Photo 53A demonstrates how to use the head as bait. Generally, the top man experiences difficulty securing the defensive man's arm in preparation for executing a guillotine. By lowering the head to where it can be grasped, the bottom man is enticed into making the mistake of reaching back to grab it. Photos 53B and 53C show the defensive wrestler making this mistake.

This set up is so sophisticated that the opponent does not immediately realize his mistake. Photo 53D shows him being rolled over into a pinning combination.

No hold or technique is complete in itself, but is valuable only when the preliminary moves necessary to set up the opponent are also known. As much time should be spent working on set ups as on any other phase of a wrestling technique. Hopefully, authors will come to recognize the necessity to include information on set ups as part of the description of how illustrated techniques are to be executed. Only in this way can these techniques be utilized to their fullest potential.

147 / BAITING AN OPPONENT

52A Leg in Lap. Lifting opponent's leg and placing it on a thigh.

52B Baiting opponent with the far leg.

SYSTEMATIC CHAMPIONSHIP WRESTLING / 148

52C Applying a pinning combination.

53A Guillotine. Lowering the head as bait.

149 / BAITING AN OPPONENT

53B   Allowing opponent to grasp the head.

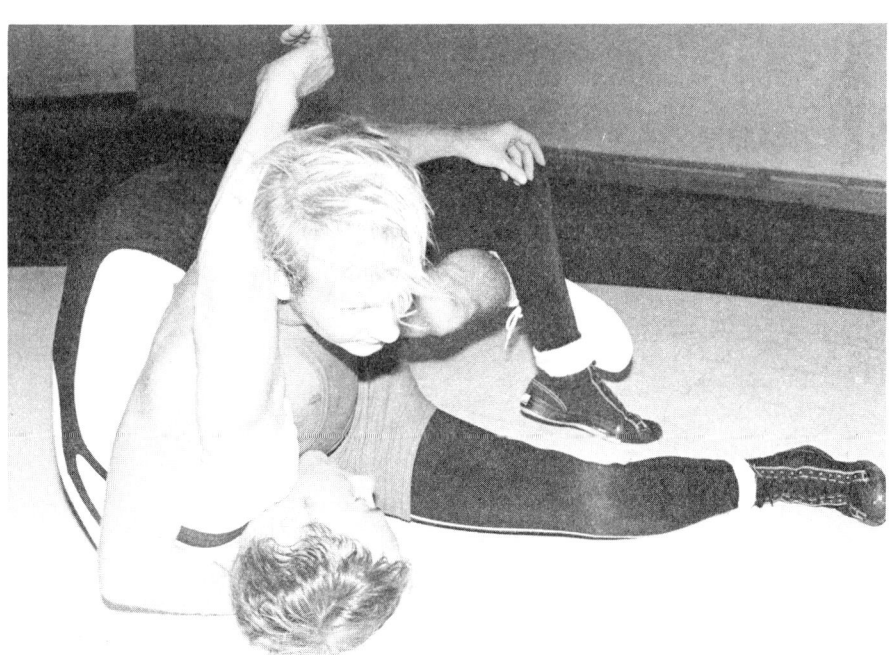

53C   Rolling over with opponent.

SYSTEMATIC CHAMPIONSHIP WRESTLING / 150

53D Applying the pinning combination.

20
Twisting Arm Fireman's Carry*

FOR COACHES WHO BELIEVE THERE IS NOTHING NEW IN WRESTLING, THE twisting arm fireman's carry offers an advanced takedown technique that is both subtle and practical and can be used effectively against even the strongest and most experienced opponents.

Studies indicate that the wrestler who takes his man down most often usually will win. Apparently, the knowledge that he can score takedowns gives him a strong psychological edge.

Interestingly, many of the most common techniques are less effective than the less common ones. The rationale is simple: the counters for the popular techniques often are perfected to the point where they are employed automatically. In short, the wrestler is conditioned to counter effectively a familiar technique by reflex.

The opponent who employs a relatively uncommon technique, such as the twisting arm fireman's carry, is thus more likely to catch an opponent by surprise. He can take advantage of opponents who have not mastered (or even practiced) suitable counter-moves.

The accompanying photographs depict the approach, contact, and follow through phases of this new technique. The offensive wrestler is wearing the dark uniform. Incidentally, the maneuver can be employed from either side depending upon the wrestler's style.

From the neutral standing position shown in photo 54A, the attacker grasps his opponent's hand with his palm down and his thumb on the outside of the opponent's wrist. Note that he wraps his hand completely around the opponent's fingers to obtain a great deal of control over the hand. The wrap around grip also makes it difficult for the defensive man to free his hand.

Next, the attacker flexes his elbow and places it inside and alongside of the opponent's forearm (photo 54B). This is the most fascinating part of the entire maneuver as it provides tremendous leverage

---

* This article reprinted with the permission of *Scholastic Coach*, May, 1971.

54A   Twisting Arm Fireman's Carry. Grasping opponent's hand.

153 / TWISTING ARM FIREMAN'S CARRY

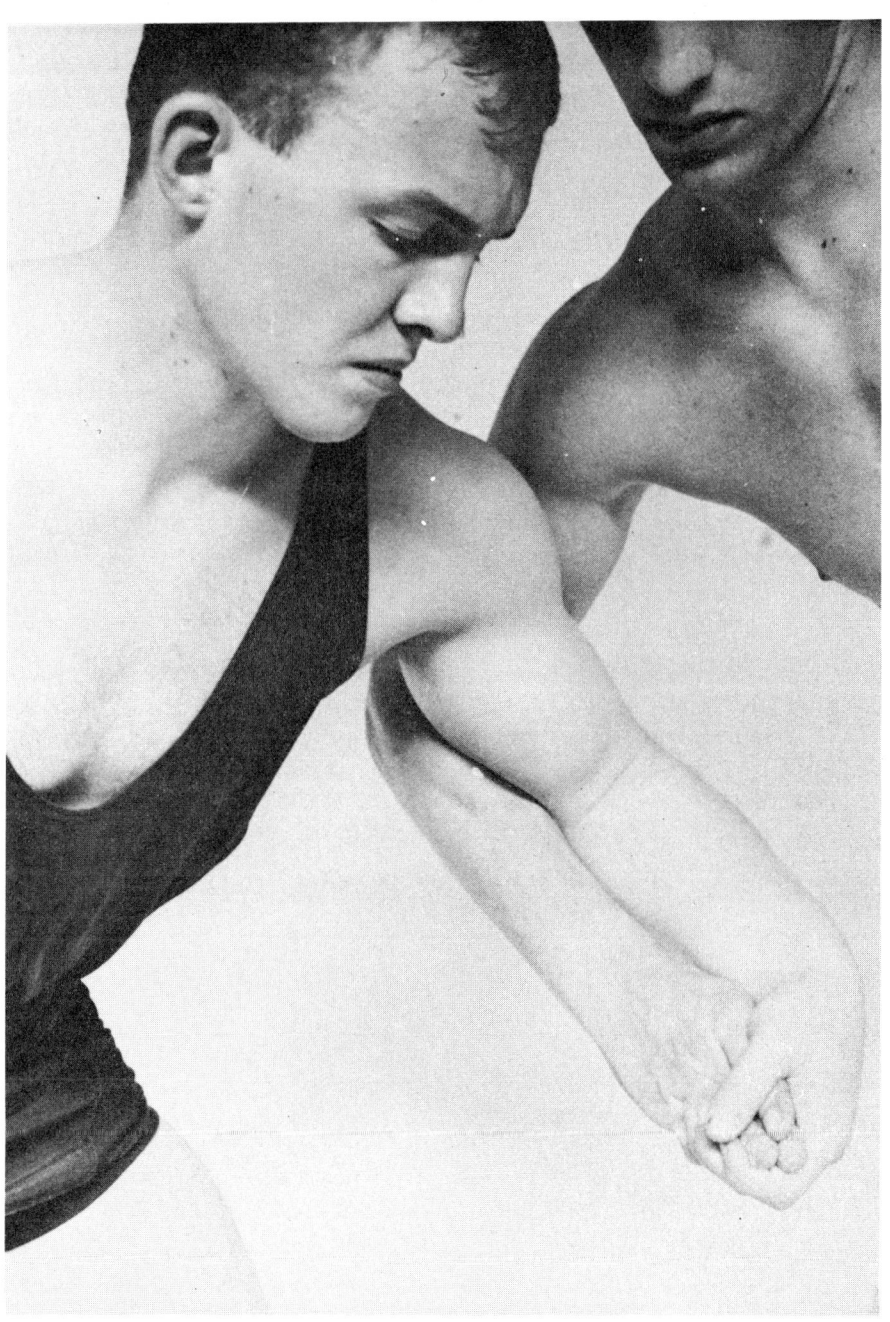

54B Placing elbow inside opponent's arm.

in controlling the opponent's arm. Regardless of the attacker's strength or skill, the amount of pressure he exerts as a result of his mechanical advantage will render his opponent's resistance virtually useless.

From this position, he drives his head forward explosively to a point underneath and beyond the opponent's armpit while maintaining the tight hold on the hand.

In photo 54C, the attacker steps between the opponent's legs while dropping his outside knee to the mat. He jams one arm into the opponent's crotch so that his weight is centered over the crook of the attacker's arm. He keeps his chest close, back straight, head high, and front of his body against the opponent's legs.

The defensive man is confronted with an impossible choice. If he drives forward or maintains his present position, he will be taken down easily. If he tries to counter by stepping backward or sprawling, he will be vulnerable to a duck-under go behind.

In photo 54D, the attacker, with the opponent's weight across the back of his sholders, easily lifts him off the mat. He merely pulls on the captured hand and lifts the arm that is between his legs. The emphasis here is on bringing the opponent's elbow and knee together.

The opponent is lowered onto his back in photo 54E. The attacker then pulls his head out from his opponent's armpit. Proper timing of this move is essential.

The attacker should not release the opponent's hand. As long as he holds on, he maintains a certain amount of control. This can be used to prevent him from turning onto his stomach.

In photo 54F, the attacker has his man in a precarious position and is ready to apply a pinning combination.

155 / TWISTING ARM FIREMAN'S CARRY

54C Dropping to one knee between opponent's legs.

SYSTEMATIC CHAMPIONSHIP WRESTLING / 156

54D Lifting opponent off the mat.

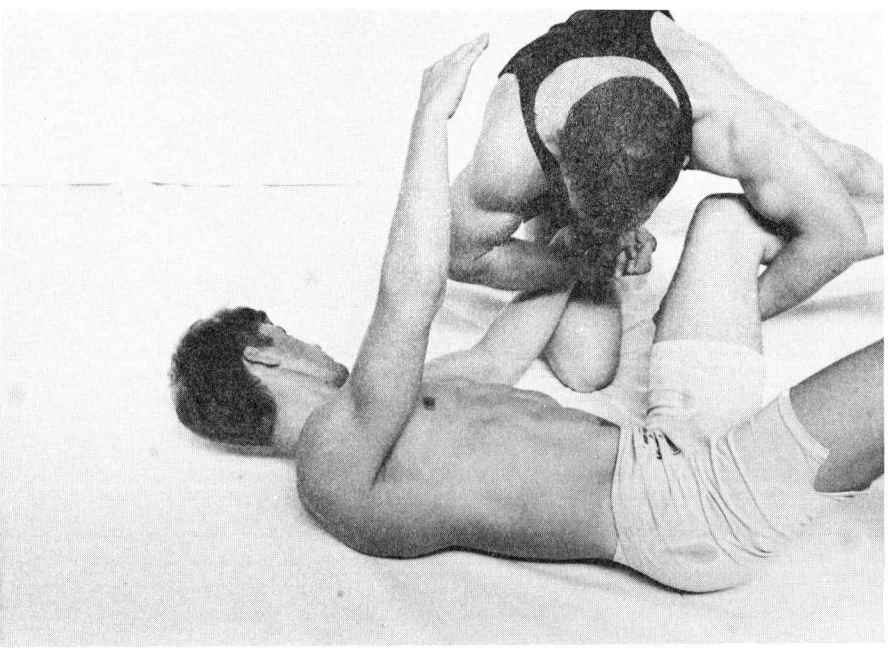

54E Lowering opponent to mat.

157 / TWISTING ARM FIREMAN'S CARRY

54F Applying a half nelson and crotch pin.

21
The Bullfighter

THE BULL TURNS, PAWS THE GROUND, AND CHARGES SPIRITEDLY. THE matador draws the bull's charge by advancing his cape, and with all the beauty and grace of a talented artist, directs the horns very closely past his body.

The matador, whether he is aware of it or not, employs certain

55A   Matador and the Bull

159 / THE BULLFIGHTER

body mechanics in molding, controlling, and eventually dominating the attacking bull. He symbolizes the triumph of finesse over force.

The two basic elements of bullfighting related to body mechanics are force and momentum. The source of force is strength. Without strength there can be no force. Without force there can be no movement.

Movement is both created and destroyed by force. The magnitude of this force is called momentum. It is the product of mass times velocity.

The bull's body constitutes mass and the speed of its movement velocity. The matador controls this unleashed force when he directs the bull's charge under the sweep of his cloak.

The movements exhibited by a matador in controlling the charging bull are similar to those which can be effectively employed in countering leg dives. This is how the technique known as the Bullfighter got its name.

When an opponent rushes in for a leg dive his momentum, like that of the charging bull, can be used to his disadvantage.

Photo 56A shows the wrestler in black attempting a leg dive. His momentum, like that of the bull, can be utilized to his disadvantage.

56A Bullfighter. Placing forearm on opponent's neck.

This is accomplished by placing a forearm against his shoulder at the side of his neck. The palm of this hand should be facing downward. The forearm acts like the matador's cape in directing the opponent's momentum.

Photo 56B shows the defending wrestler moving out to the side of the rushing opponent. By positioning himself to one side, he gains the mechanical advantage in reducing the amount of expected resistance. The disadvantage that would have been incurred by remaining in the path of the oncoming opponent is thereby avoided.

In photo 56C, the absence of a sufficient resistive force combined with the impetus of the opponent's momentum has forced him onto his hands and knees. While on all fours, it is difficult for him to keep the man on top from pivoting to a position of advantage. As long as the top man's weight is over him with his legs back out of reach, he cannot easily be kept from spinning around to one side.

The Bullfighter is completed in photo 56D when the bottom man is broken down and a pinning combination applied.

Leg dives are the most popularly employed means of gaining takedowns. It is therefore essential that an effective counter be employed.

56B Moving out to one side of rushing opponent.

161 / THE BULLFIGHTER

56C Pivoting to a position of advantage.

56D Breaking opponent down to mat.

The natural reaction would be to shoot the legs back, spreading them wide apart; this not only brings the legs farther from the opponent's arms as he attempts to grasp them, but also gives a wider platform, which the opponent will have more difficulty upsetting. Admittedly, by getting the center of gravity back away from the opponent, it becomes more difficult or maybe even impossible to be lifted off the mat. However, this reaction is more of a block than a counter. It is strictly defensive.

By remaining in the path of the charging opponent, a great deal of energy is expended simply to halt his charge. It would be wiser to put this energy to better use by avoiding the charge in working toward gaining the position of advantage.

Momentum should never be worked against directly. It is unwise to directly oppose a moving opponent. It is much wiser to gain an angle that allows for a distant advantage. In this way, the opponent's momentum can be used against him once contact is made.

A leg drive can be countered most effectively when the laws of movement mechanics are applied. This necessitates placing the body in such a position that the least resistance will be created. Force should then be exerted from an angle so as to parry the opponent's momentum. Less energy is required to divert momentum than is required to overpower it.

22
Taking an Opponent Down from Behind

A STANDING WRESTLER IN THE POSITION OF DISADVANTAGE MUST BE TAKEN down to the mat if he is to be effectively controlled. While standing, he has advantages not possessed while on the mat. He is more mobile, for example. He can move faster and with less effort. Consequently, he is harder to control.

The defensive wrestler can only be scored upon when his shoulders come close to or in actual contact with the surface of the mat. While standing he cannot be scored against.

Another advantage of standing is that it is less tiring. Weight cannot be put on a wrestler while he is standing. He cannot be made to carry the burden of carrying the offensive man's weight.

Methods of taking an opponent to the mat from behind oftentimes require encircling his waist. The fingers of both hands are commonly curled and locked together in one of three types of grips. The following photos show close-ups of each of these grips.

A popular method of taking an opponent to the mat is the tilt (photo 60A). It is executed by bringing pressure to bear on the defensive man's stomach. Squeezing tightly insures that control of the body is maintained. The opponent is then elevated from the mat by thrusting the hips forward and arching the back. The technique is completed by turning him sideways and returning him to the mat.

More strength is required in employing this technique than most others. A considerable amount of caution must also be exercised in returning him to the mat with a reasonable degree of gentleness.

The second method of taking an opponent to the mat from behind is the forward trip (photo 61A). It is most effectively employed when the opponent is leaning forward. A leg should be wrapped around one of his legs. Then by sweeping the leg back while pushing forward with the chest and shoulder he is brought down to the mat.

SYSTEMATIC CHAMPIONSHIP WRESTLING / 164

The third method of bringing an opponent back to the mat is the whirl (photo 62A). This is simplest to employ when the opponent is motionless. It is executed from either side. One foot is placed behind the heel of the defensive man. Simultaneously, the weight is thrown backward. Timing is very important.

As the defensive man falls, he should be whirled around 180 degrees so that he lands on his stomach. When he strikes the mat, a quick turn should be made to maintain the position of advantage on top.

In order to reduce further the possibility of losing the position of advantage, one of the defensive man's arms should be firmly gripped on the way down to the mat. Control of the arm will prevent him from executing a switch counter.

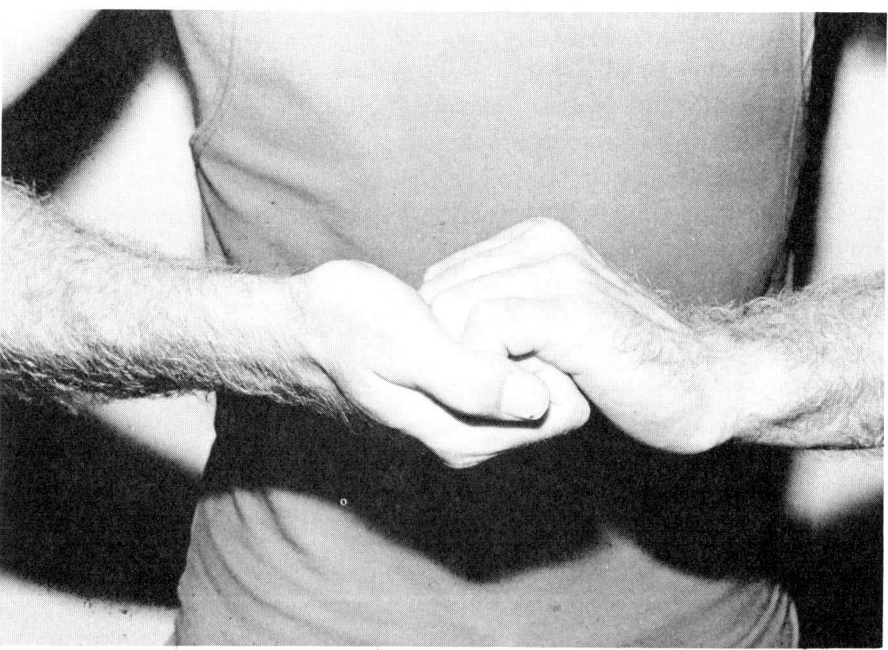

57A Grip "A." This type of grip is formed by hooking the fingers of both hands together and turning the thumbs in to protect them when making contact with the mat.

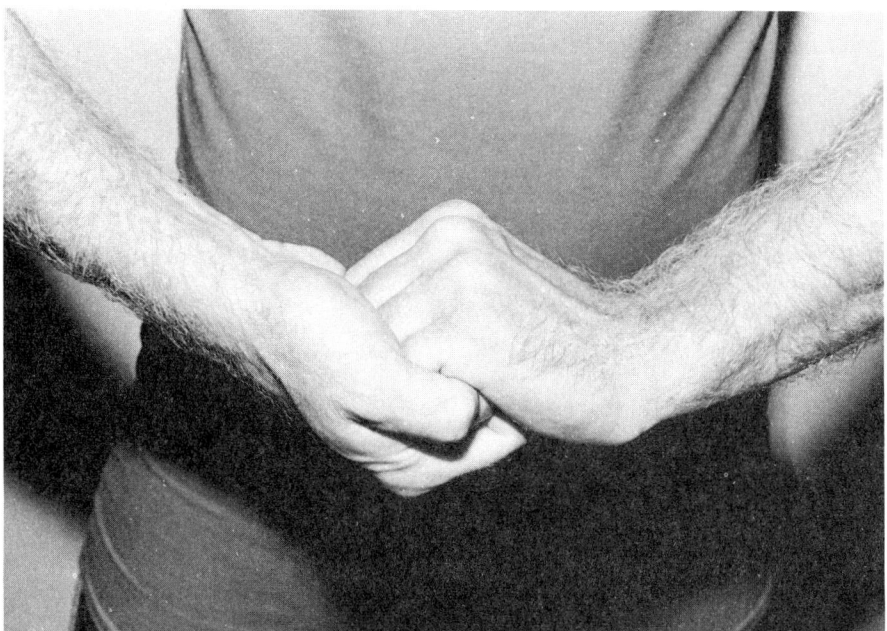

58A Grip "B." This grip is secured by bending the fingers and thumbs at right angles. In this position, they are cupped. The palm of one hand is faced downward while the other is turned upward so it is at right angles to the other. The thumbs and fingers are then locked together.

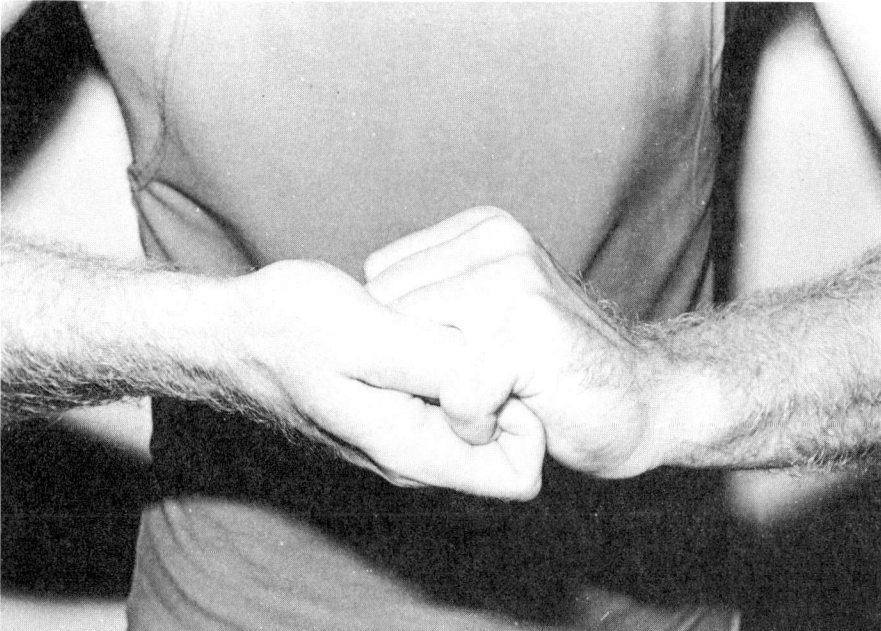

59A Grip "C." This grip is commonly referred to as the wrestler's grip. It is obtained by placing the thumb of one hand between the fourth and fifth fingers of the opposite hand. The advantage of this grip is that none of the fingertips are exposed for the opponent to grab onto.

60A Tilt

61A Forward Trip

62A Whirl

Part V
ESCAPES AND REVERSALS

23
Why the Stand-Up Is So Popular in Collegiate Wrestling

THE STAND-UP IS THE MOST POPULAR ESCAPE EMPLOYED IN COLLEGE wrestling. Research covering sixteen years of N.C.A.A. championship wrestling shows that it is attempted more often than any other escape or reversal. Despite its popularity it is not the most effective escape.

The table below shows that out of the 592 recorded attempts, it was successful only 179 times. In other words, it failed to gain points seven out of every ten times it was tried.

In contrast to this, the sit-out, percentage-wise, was more effective. It succeeded four out of every ten times it was attempted.

TABLE 3

Frequency and General Effectiveness of the Three Most Commonly Employed Escape and Reversal Techniques in Sixteen Years of N.C.A.A. Championship Matches

Escapes and Reversals	Number of Attempts	Number of Attempts Resulting in Points Gained	Number of Attempts Resulting in Points Lost
Stand-up	592	179	1
Sit-out	174	66	7
Switch	132	28	0

The puzzling question is why the stand-up is more popular than other techniques. Several factors may be responsible. There is, for example, less of a risk involved in using a stand-up than is true for most other escapes. Of the 592 times it was attempted, there was only one instance when it lost points for the wrestler attempting it. The sit-out, however, was successfully countered seven out of the 174 times it was tried. Two of these seven counters resulted in falls and cost the wrestlers national championships.

Some wrestling techniques are too risky to wisely be attempted under the present rules. The rules are set up so that there is basically only one way a wrestler in the bottom position can lose points: if one or both of his shoulders come in contact with or are close to the surface of the mat. The smart wrestler will, therefore, come up off the mat as often as possible. Standing is the safest position. While standing, his shoulders are the farthest possible from the mat. The odds favor his standing as opposed to being down on the mat.

Most escape and reversal techniques, which are employed from down on the mat, can also be employed from standing. The only difference is that when executed from a standing position, there is less of a risk of losing points if they are countered.

The farther the shoulders are kept from the mat the harder it is for an opponent to score points. A mistake made four feet above the mat is of little consequence. However, the same mistake made four inches from the mat surface may cost the wrestler the match.

Another equally good reason for the popularity of the stand up is that after gaining a standing position, the wrestler only has to carry his own weight and not that of his opponent. This reduces his energy expenditure, and makes it possible for him to employ that energy in attempting to get away. It also enables him to shift his weight easily in maintaining balance. The less weight he has to carry the easier it is to escape. By forcing his opponent to carry the burden of his own body weight, the opponent will likely tire sooner.

Another advantage of standing is mobility. The wrestler is most mobile in a standing position. His capacity to move fast is much greater while standing than in any other position. While standing, he is harder to control. On the mat he is at a distinct disadvantage. inasmuch as his maneuverability is vastly decreased.

There are basically three methods of standing up. They are: (1) by bringing the outside leg forward, (2) by bringing the inside leg forward, (3) by bringing both legs forward at the same time, and (4) by bringing the weight of the body back over both legs.

Each of these methods of standing up requires that the head be held high, the back be kept straight, and the elbows be tucked in tightly to the sides of the body. These moves are necessary in order to be assured that there is a strong supporting base from which to work.

The initial sequence of movements employed in performing the bump back stand-up illustrated in photos 63A through 63C.

While gaining altitude (in coming up to a standing position), the chest should be lifted high, the spine kept straight, and the opponent's hand removed from the elbow (photo 63D). For maximum

173 / WHY THE STAND-UP IS SO POPULAR

control, the fingers of the opponent's hand should be cupped while it is being forced back (photo 63E).

The captured hand should be placed behind the body while taking a firm grip of the hand that is around the waist (photo 63F).

The hand on the waist should be peeled off while moving out away from the opponent. A firm grip should be maintained until after pivoting to face the opponent (photo 63G).

The following is a list of fundamentals that should be adhered to regardless of which method of standing up is employed:

1. Always keep the head up and back straight;
2. Always use two hands to control one of the opponent's;
3. Always keep the feet moving in short choppy steps;
4. Always keep the elbows close to the sides of the body;
5. Always keep plenty of mat space ahead of you.

Some of the things that should be avoided when standing up are:

1. Never bring the hips up first;
2. Never swing the arms out away from the sides of the body;
3. Never spread the legs;

63A Bump Back Stand Up. Starting referee's position.

SYSTEMATIC CHAMPIONSHIP WRESTLING / 174

4. Never stand still;
5. Never move in a straight line.

Most escapes from down on the mat can also be used from standing. However, there is less of a risk when they are employed from standing. This plus the fact that standing up is less tiring and has fewer limitations on mobility accounts for its popularity in collegiate wrestling.

63B   Pushing back to a squatting position.

63C Keeping the arms in close to the sides of the body.

63D Removing opponent's hand from the elbow while coming up to standing.

177 / WHY THE STAND-UP IS SO POPULAR

63E Forcing opponent's hand to the rear.

63F Grasping opponent's other hand.

179 / WHY THE STAND-UP IS SO POPULAR

63G   Pivoting to face opponent.

24
The Short Sit-Out: A Dangerous Wrestling Technique

A CRITICAL ANALYSIS OF THE RELATIVE EFFECTIVENESS OF ALL ESCAPE and reversal techniques employed in the N.C.A.A. championship wrestling matches from 1952 to 1955 and from 1956 to 1969 indicates that the short sit-out is the one technique that requires the defensive wrestler to take the greatest risk in losing points if it is successfully countered. In other words, according to this research study, the short sit-out is the one escape technique that is most likely to lose points for the wrestler attempting it.

The success of a wrestler or of an entire wrestling team is dependent to a large extent upon the effectiveness of the escape techniques taught by the coach. The general practice has been for most coaches to teach those techniques which in their opinions, based on past experience, were most effective for them. While the majority of the techniques selected by coaches are effective part of the times they are employed, many are, however, of doubtful value. One such technique is the short sit-out.

The defensive wrestler, in photo 64A, while executing the short sit-out, is in a precarious position since he has very little support to his back side. In this position, there is a danger of being pulled over onto his back as is illustrated in photo 65. Also, while in this sitting position, the defensive wrestler has very limited mobility. This limitation on movement is a result of unstable posture and balance.

Coaches would be wise to teach techniques that have been used most successfully by champions. The short sit-out is definitely not one of them. In sixteen years of championship matches in N.C.A.A. competition, the short sit-out has lost points or the match for the offensive wrestler on seven occasions while gaining only 66 points

---

* This article reprinted with the permission of *Scholastic Wrestling News*, February 15, 1970.

181 / THE SHORT SIT-OUT

64A Short Sit-Out

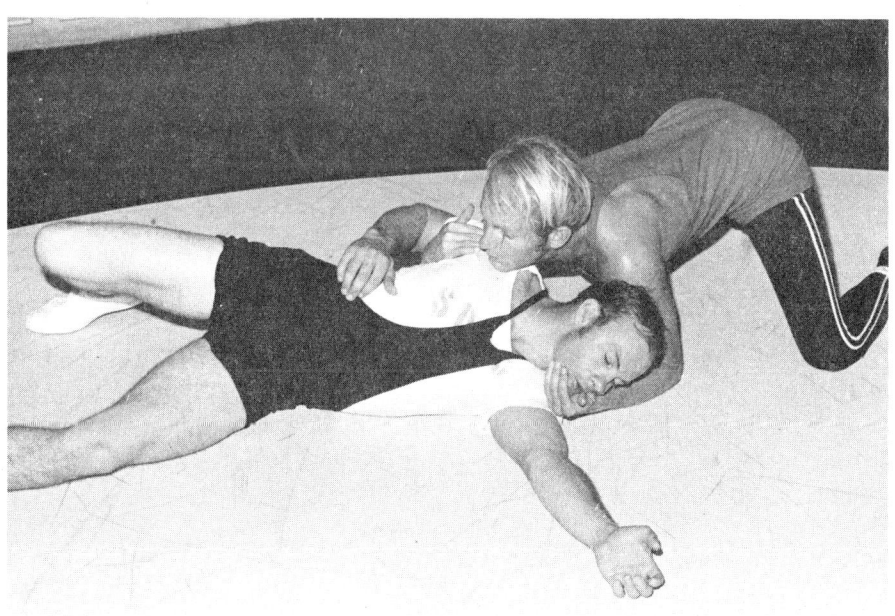

65A Short Sit-Out Counter

in 174 attempts, 15 points (five near-falls) and two national championships for those wrestlers attempting it.

Some coaches will teach techniques that can be executed successfully against beginners and opponents of poor caliber, but when these same techniques are employed against stronger, more experienced competitors they prove to be ineffective. The chances of these techniques being successfully countered is high.

A certain amount of discretion should be exercised in the selection of the techniques taught. Since the primary interest of coaches is to get the most positive results from the time and effort invested, techniques of dubious merit, such as the short sit-out, should be avoided. In order to do the most to complement their efforts to produce winning teams, coaches have to consider not only those techniques which have the greatest chance of gaining points, but also those which are the most likely not to lose points if they are successfully countered. A minimum recommendation in terms of teaching the short sit-out would be that if it is attempted, it should be done with the utmost caution since the risk of losing points appears to be greater than any other escape technique. The main purpose for teaching the technique might be to practice a counter for it. Its use, however, as an escape technique should be discouraged. Discouraging the use of the short sit-out is best accomplished by teaching an effective counter before the technique is mastered. If the counter is emphasized before the skill is executed proficiently, it will not likely be included in the wrestlers' repertoire.

The short sit-out counter illustrated in photo 65A is employed in the following manner. When the offensive wrestler completes the sit through to the sitting position, the defensive wrestler drops his right hand over his opponent's right shoulder, grasping his chin, while bringing his left hand, which is around his opponent's waist, to a position under his opponent's left armpit. He carries his head to the left of his opponent's head. This, then, checks his opponent in a sitting position. Now the opponent is jerked backward with a sudden pull of both hands. While being pulled backward, the opponent's chin is snapped to the right. This counter is commonly referred to as an arm lock and chin cup, or drop back.

25
Stand-Up with Hand Control

THE KEY TO EXECUTING AN EFFICIENT STAND-UP LIES IN CONTROLLING the opponent's hands. This is the most important single factor in successfully escaping by means of the stand-up.

The stand-up escape is commonly countered when the offensive wrestler succeeds in his attempts to lock his hands around the bottom man's waist. With proper hand control, the opponent can be prevented from locking his hands. Starting in the referee's position, the bottom man should adhere to certain fundamentals. He should keep his head up and back straight. His weight should never be over his hands. This tends to anchor them to the mat. Instead, the weight should be set back over the haunches. This permits the hands to be moved freely. The toes should be curled under. This provides for a springlike coil action in raising from the mat. Keeping the hands turned in slightly, with the elbows bent, also assists in moving explosively to a standing posture (photo 66A).

Regardless of the type of stand-up employed, hand control should always be initiated by bringing the inside arm back to a position against the side of the body. The upper part of the arm should be held tightly to the flank so no space exists between the arm and the body. When the opponent reaches over the arm, he can be prevented from joining his hands by moving the arm away from the side of the body. If he draws his hand back and tries to place it between the body and the extended arm, the arm simply needs to be brought back to the side of the body. While the opponent is attempting to interlock his hands, the far arm should be brought across in front of the body in order to grasp the fingers of his hand (photo 66B).

While holding the opponent's fingers out away from the body, the other hand should be used to reach up and regrasp the fingers with both hands (photo 66C). This is hand control. It involves using two hands to control the opponent's one hand. Two on one permits the opponent's hand to be forced back behind the body (photo 66D).

66A   Inside Leg Stand-Up. Starting referee's position.

66B Stepping forward with the inside leg.

66C   Forcing opponent's hand behind the body.

66D Removing opponent's hand from around the waist.

66E Turning to face opponent.

67A Stand-Up (Incorrect Method #1). Creating a space between the side of the body and the arm is a mistake.

The opponent now has only one arm around the waist. In this position, it is impossible for him to prevent an escape. The escape is completed by retaining a grip on the hand that is behind the back while turning to face him (photo 66E). The turn should be made by pivoting quickly.

When standing up, it is not necessary to initially grab for the hand that is around the waist. Grabbing this hand would be a mistake since it creates a space between the arm and the side of the body. This is illustrated in photo 67A.

The hand that is on the elbow is the only one to be concerned about. It is this hand and not the one around the waist that will determine whether the opponent will be successful in locking his hands about the waist.

If the opponent is successful in locking his hands around the waist, his hold will most likely have to be forcibly broken by separating his hands (photo 68A). To separate his hands, a strong crouching posture has to be retained while lifting one hand, pushing down the other hand, and simultaneously pulling them apart (photo 68B).

A stand up should be employed any time an opponent does not

SYSTEMATIC CHAMPIONSHIP WRESTLING / 190

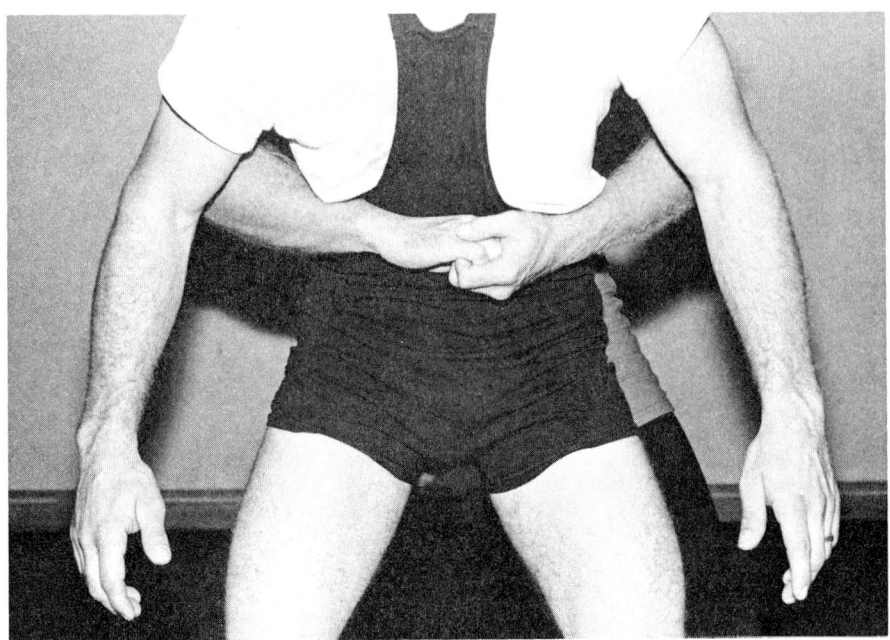

68A Standing Rear Body Lock Counter. Having opponent's arms locked around the waist.

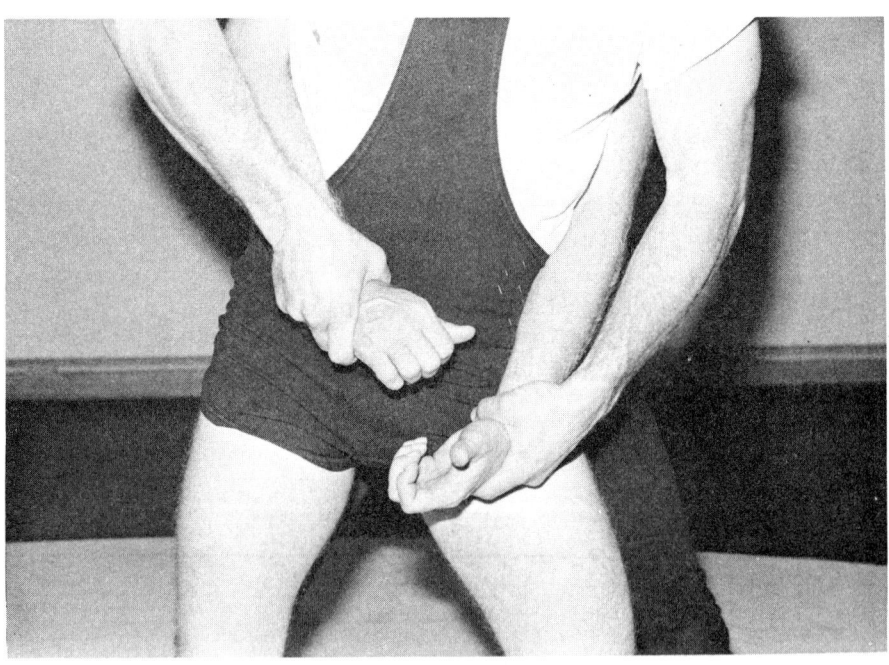

68B Separating opponent's locked hands.

191 / STAND-UP WITH HAND CONTROL

69A Stand-Up (Incorrect Method #2). Rising to a standing position improperly by neglecting to keep the elbow tucked into the side of the body.

control the legs. Standing up is the least dangerous move, since it is most hard to control a wrestler on his feet.

The best defense from underneath is to come up to standing. This must be done while keeping the inside elbow tucked in to the side of the body, and not in the manner illustrated in photo 69A.

It is advisable to keep the body perpendicular while getting to a standing position. This prevents the opponent from employing a cradle counter. The incorrect way of raising from the mat with the head held low is illustrated in photo 70A.

When coming up off the mat, the shoulders should be thrown back to relieve the burden of the opponent's weight. Rise quickly, keeping the spine straight. The feet should be spread, the knees bent, and the body low.

Emphasis should be on gaining control of the offensive man's hands. It is foolish to have to work to break an opponent's grip when he could initially be prevented from locking his hands.

After having come up to a standing position, the bottom man should run forward in short choppy steps in order to keep the opponent from being able to reach down and grasp a leg. The pattern

70A Stand-Up (Incorrect Method #3). Failing to keep head high while coming to a standing position.

of running should be circular so as not to be forced off the edge of the mat.

The stand-up is the least exhausting escape technique that can be employed from the referee's position. Unlike other escapes, the wrestler does not have the weight of the top man on his back. This provides for greater freedom of movement and maneuverability minus the burden and hindrance created by an opponent's additional weight.

The disadvantage of carrying an opponent's weight is the higher energy cost. Excess weight causes early fatigue. The sooner a wrestler tires the less efficient will be his efforts to escape. Carrying an opponent around on his back drains his energy and eventually costs him points. It is best to stay up and off the mat.

The stand-up is the safest escape technique that can be attempted, since it places the wrestler's shoulders the greatest possible distance from the mat.

Most escape maneuvers that are attempted on or near the surface of the mat are too risky to attempt under the present rules. As long as points are awarded in accordance with the proximity of the shoulders to the mat surface, it is wisest to come up off the mat as soon and as often as possible.

26
Standing Versus on the Mat Escapes and Reversals*

DURING THE PAST YEAR, THE AUTHOR COMPLETED A STUDY ON THE RELAtive effectiveness of escape and reversal techniques performed in the N.C.A.A. wrestling championships from 1952 to 1969, excluding 1955.

One of the most significant conclusions was that the standing position offers a safer option than the mat position on any escape or reversal, which can be executed from either position. The wrestler who effects the move from the standing position will be less likely to lose points.

The accompanying table offers a comparison between identical escape and reversal techniques as performed standing and from the mat, with respect to the percentage of attempts that resulted in no loss of points.

TABLE 4

Comparison Between Identical Escape and Reversal Techniques Performed from Mat and Standing Positions at N.C.A.A. Championships from 1952 to 1969 (Except 1955)

Escape or Reversal Technique	Percentage of Attempts Resulting in no points Being Lost
Stand-up-turn	99.8
Sit-out-turn	96.0
Stand-up-switch	100.0
Switch	100.0
Stand-up-roll	100.0
Side-roll	98.3
Stand-up-shoulder-roll	100.0
Shoulder-roll	98.2
Stand-up-whizzer	100.0
Whizzer	95.6

* This article reprinted with the permission of *Scholastic Coach*, May, 1970.

The data clearly favored the standing position. When skills such as the side-roll, shoulder-roll, and whizzer were attempted from the standing position, they never lost points for the defensive wrestler, whereas when they were attempted on the mat, a definite percentage of them did lose points for the performer.

From this, we can deduce that the height at which execution is effected can be considered a sound basis for the selection of escape and reversal techniques.

The wrestler in the underneath or defensive position must attempt either an escape or reversal in order to gain points. He has the option of many techniques, several of which can be attempted from either a standing position or on the mat.

Each option possesses a varying chance of success and a varying amount of risk. Some obviously are riskier than others. Many have approximately an equal chance of success. But the least risky options are those which can be performed from a standing position, as the wrestler will be in a higher position than his opponent throughout the move. Chances are that a mistake four feet above the mat won't cost him points, whereas a mistake one to four inches off the mat could cost him two or three points.

The problem of deciding which technique to use to get free or gain a position of advantage can be a difficult one for a wrestler who is unfamiliar with the relative effectiveness of his techniques. The smart wrestler will play the percentages. He won't gamble unless the situation leaves him little choice. That means he won't attempt any technique from the mat that can be done standing, unless time is running out and he is behind in the score.

Whenever such a technique is performed from on the mat (instead of from standing), the athlete should exercise greater caution, as the risk of losing points is greater. The good wrestlers play the percentages as much as possible during the entire match and resort to gambling only when the situation warrants a calculated risk.

The most effective escape and reversal techniques are those which gain points most of the time and rarely lose points when they are countered: in short, the techniques which are both the most successful and the safest.

The following five techniques are illustrated from the standing position, though they can also be performed from on the mat: (1) the stand-up-turn (commonly called the sit-out-turn done on the mat), (2) the stand-up-side-roll (the side-roll on the mat), (3) the stand-up-switch, (4) the stand-up-whizzer, and (5) the stand-up-shoulder-roll (the switch, the whizzer, and the shoulder-roll on the mat).

Their execution from the standing position assures the wrestler of the least amount of risk from successful counters.

Stand-up Turn

The defensive wrestler begins by shoving off from the mat with both hands, throwing his weight back upon his knees and feet, gaining height by lifting his chest high, and immediately grabbing the hands of his opponent. With a quick decisive movement, he spreads the opponent's hands apart, freeing himself, and turns to face the opponent.

71A Stand-Up-Turn

197 / ESCAPES AND REVERSALS

72A   Sit-Out-Turn

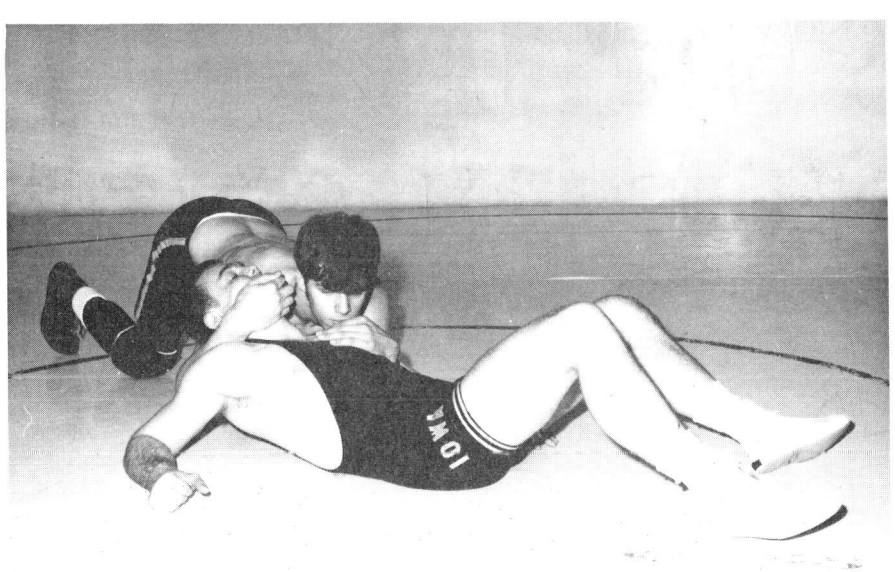

73A   Counter to Sit-Out-Turn

Stand-up-side-roll

The wrestler wraps his right arm around the opponent's right arm, above the elbow. He then drops his left leg back on the mat to the outside of his man's right leg and rolls forward over his right shoulder at an angle of 45 degrees, carrying the opponent with him by pulling on his right arm. He lands with his body perpendicular to his opponent and his back on the opponent's chest, and then makes a quick turn toward the opponent's legs.

74A   Stand-Up-Side-Roll

199 / ESCAPES AND REVERSALS

75A   Side-Roll

76A   Counter to Side-Roll

Stand-up-switch

The wrestler grasps his opponent's right hand with his right hand while placing his left palm against the inside of the opponent's right thigh. With his right arm over the opponent's right arm, the wrestler is now able to force his opponent down flat on the mat by simply sitting down. Once on the mat, he should move on top of the opponent's back by turning to his right and swinging his left arm around the man.

77A   Stand-Up-Switch

201 / ESCAPES AND REVERSALS

78A Switch

79A Counter to Switch

Stand-up-whizzer

The wrestler swings his left arm back over his head to the top of the opponent's right bicep. He exerts pressure down onto the man's shoulder joint and then turns in facing his opponent to effect an escape.

80A Stand-Up-Whizzer

203 / ESCAPES AND REVERSALS

81A Whizzer

82A Counter to Whizzer

SYSTEMATIC CHAMPIONSHIP WRESTLING / 204

Stand-up-shoulder-roll

The wrestler bends forward sharply at the waist while tucking his chin to his chest. He then forcefully drives off one of his feet while kicking the other over his buttocks, enabling him to somersault to a position in front of his opponent.

83A   Stand-Up-Shoulder-Roll

205 / ESCAPES AND REVERSALS

84A Shoulder-Roll

85A Counter to Shoulder-Roll

27
Standing Chain Wrestling

STANDING CHAIN WRESTLING CAN BE DEFINED AS A SERIES OF TECHNIQUES executed from a defensive standing position in a continuous manner in accordance with the movements of an opponent. It entails linking, putting together, or coupling individual isolated techniques into a uniform uninterrupted series. Any technique executed with the full intent of making it successful and with the insight into predicting blocks and counters can be employed in chain wrestling.

Insight into various combinations makes it possible to execute secondary moves utilizing the opponent's weakened position resulting from his having blocked or countered an initial technique.

Wrestlers often stop after attempting one escape or reversal. By failing to attempt another technique immediately the opponent is given time to adjust and prepare to block or counter the next move. If such a large gap of time elapses between a wrestler's initial move and his subsequent moves, the opponent will likely have little difficulty blocking or countering each one individually. Consequently, the effectiveness of any escape or reversal pattern is destroyed.

Seldom is success realized by attempting one isolated technique. This is particularly true as the level of ability in competition increases. Highly competitive matches, almost without exception, entail several successive techniques being countered before one is successful. Isolated techniques are rarely successful in top-notch competition.

Techniques are valuable only when combined. By themselves they are, in general, of little worth. None is complete in itself, but of value primarily when integrated into a sequence.

Chain wrestling requires building techniques upon other techniques. It is dependent upon continuity and sequence of movement. Only by merging techniques into some sort of chain or series can the most positive results be realized.

Three common methods of coming up to a standing position are presented below.

207 / STANDING CHAIN WRESTLING

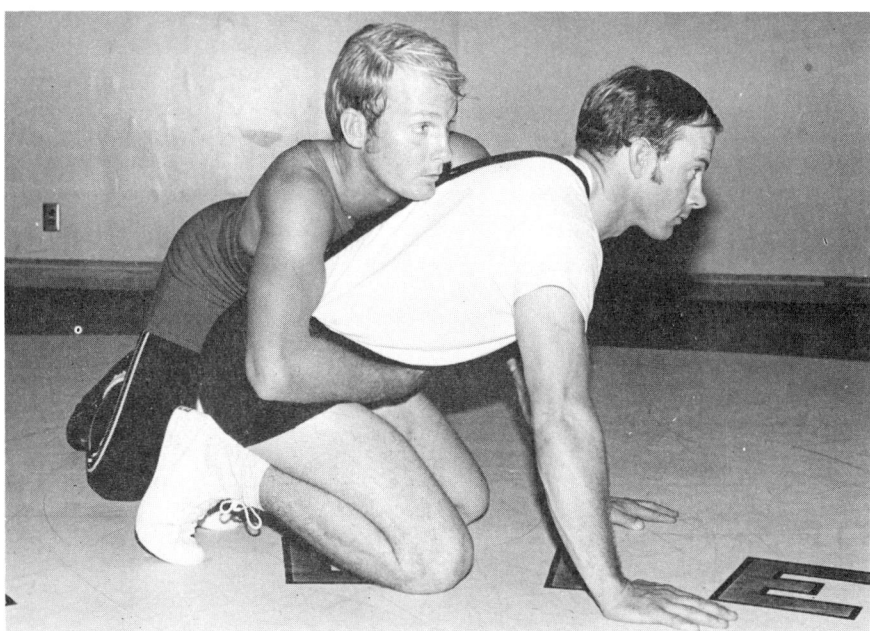

86A Outside Leg Stand Up. Keeping the toes tucked under, head up, the palms turned inward in the referee's position.

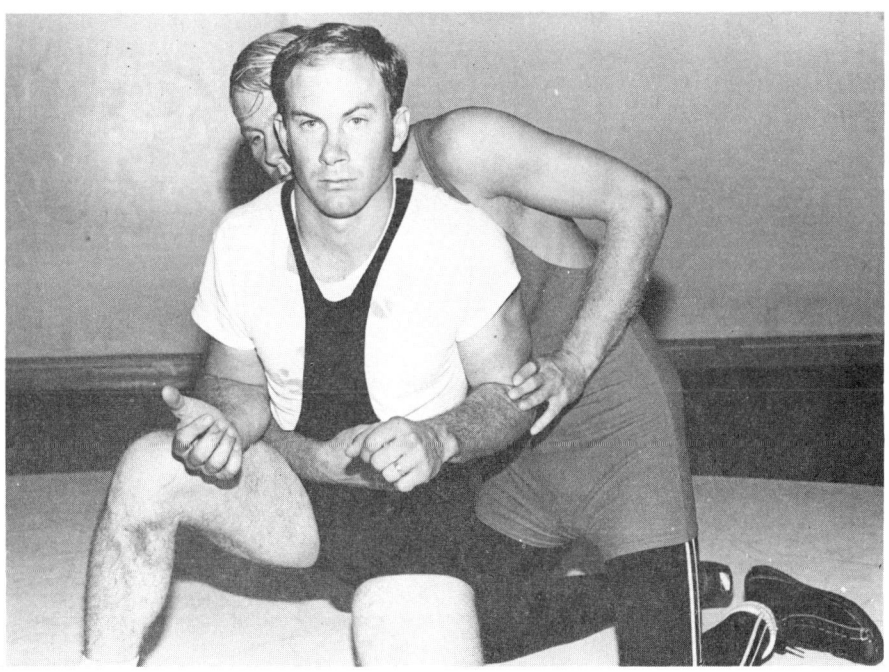

86B Stepping forward with the outside leg while bringing the inside arm back against the side of the body.

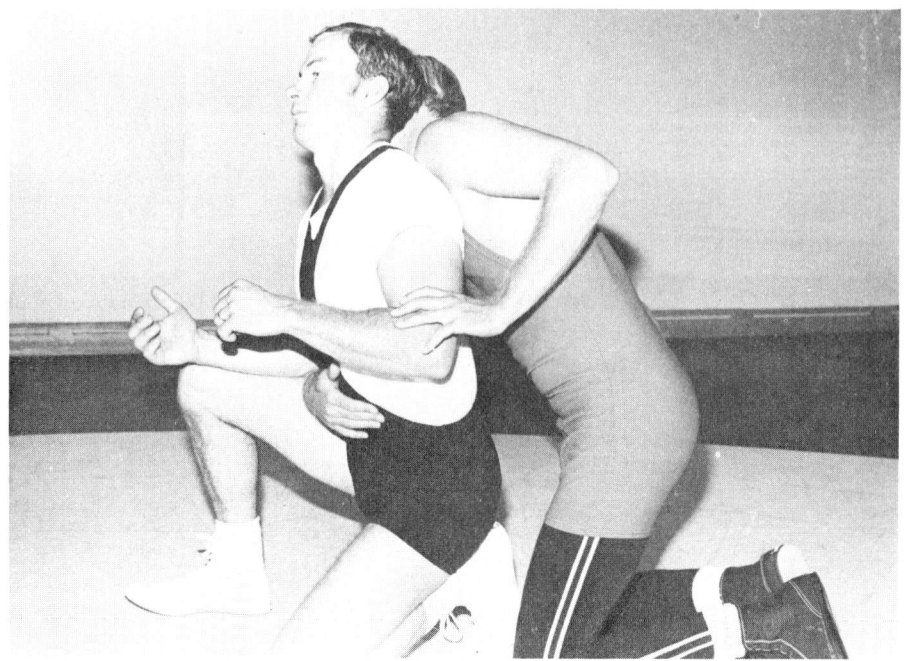

86C Keeping the back straight while moving up.

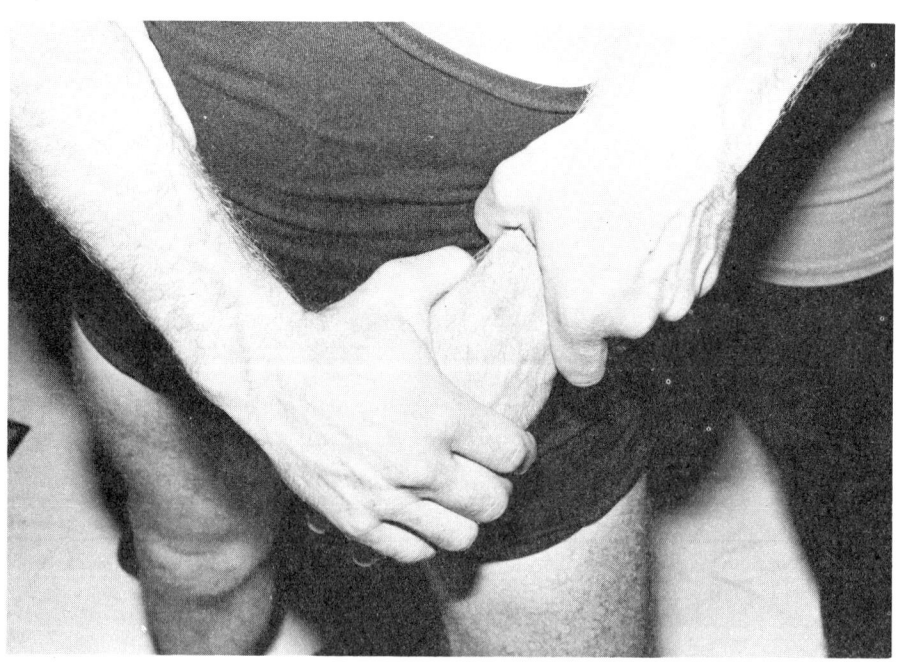

86D Placing two hands on opponent's one hand.

86E Removing the hand from around the waist while turning and moving away.

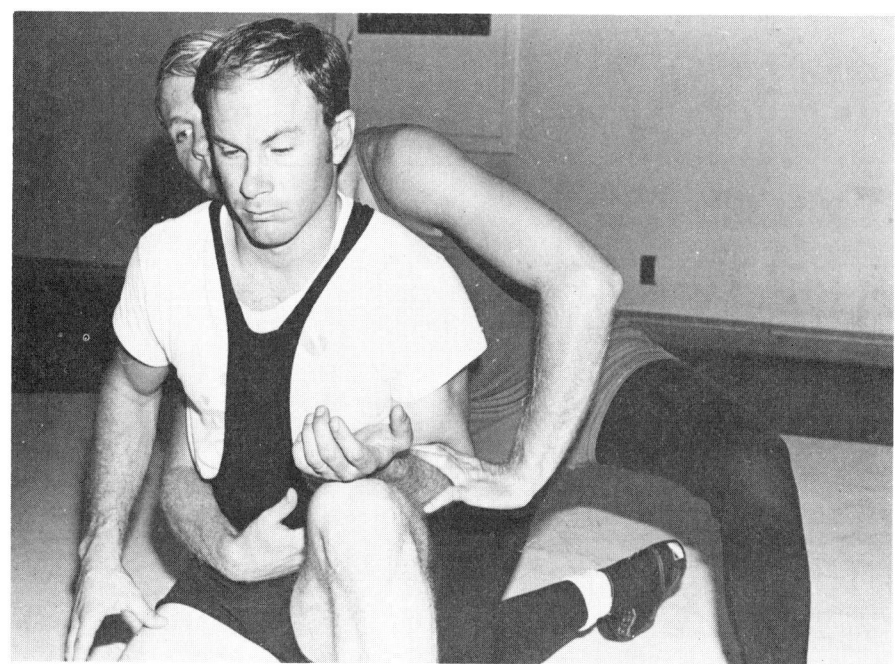

87A Inside Leg Stand Up. Bringing the inside arm back against the side of the body to prevent opponent from locking his arms around the waist while stepping forward with inside leg.

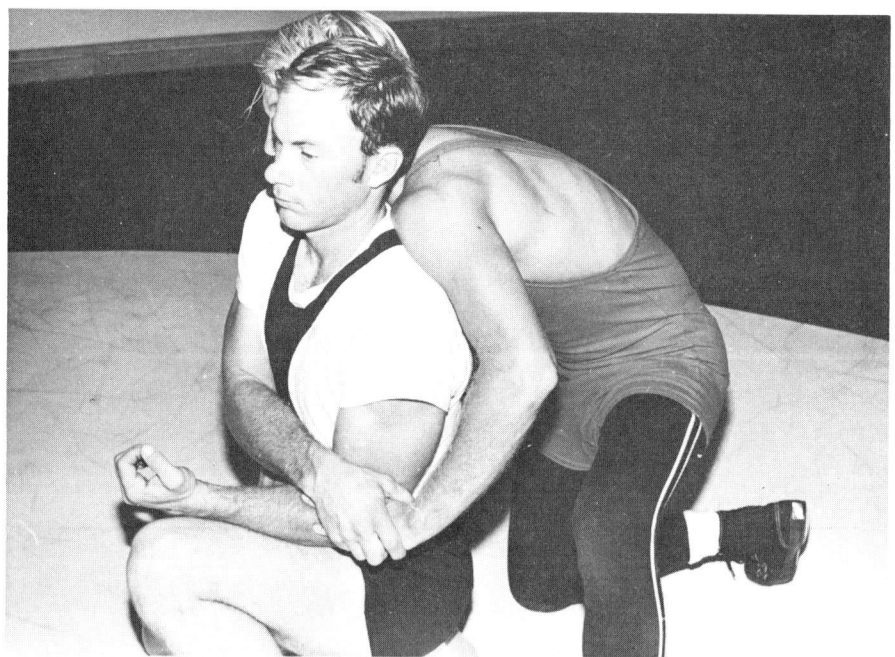

87B Reaching across to grasp opponent's hand.

211 / STANDING CHAIN WRESTLING

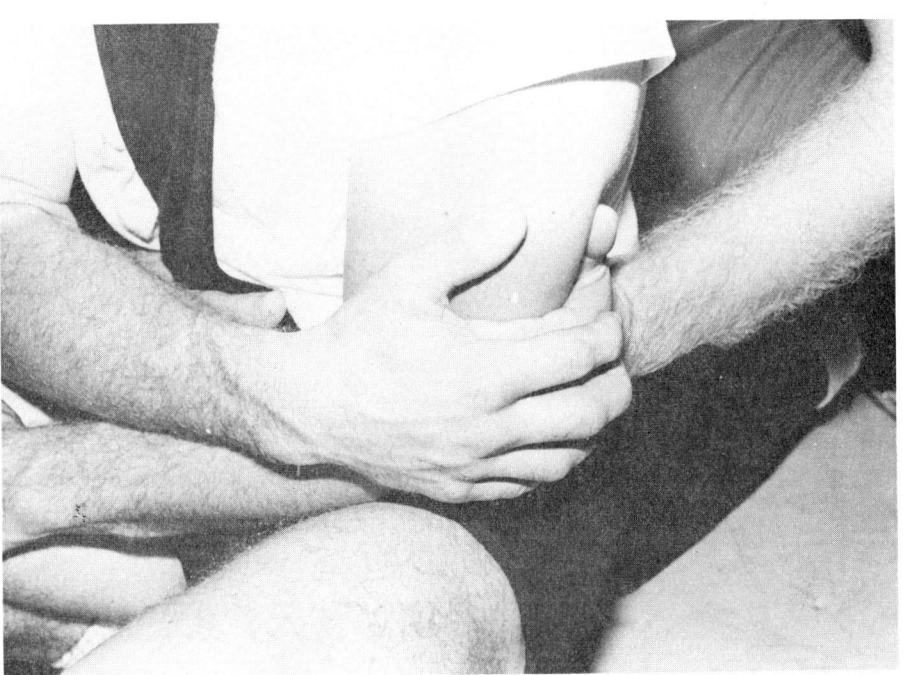

87C Securing a firm grip on opponent's hand.

87D Coming up to standing while forcing opponent's hand back.

213 / STANDING CHAIN WRESTLING

87E Continuing to force hand to the rear while reaching for the hand that is around the waist prior to turning to face opponent.

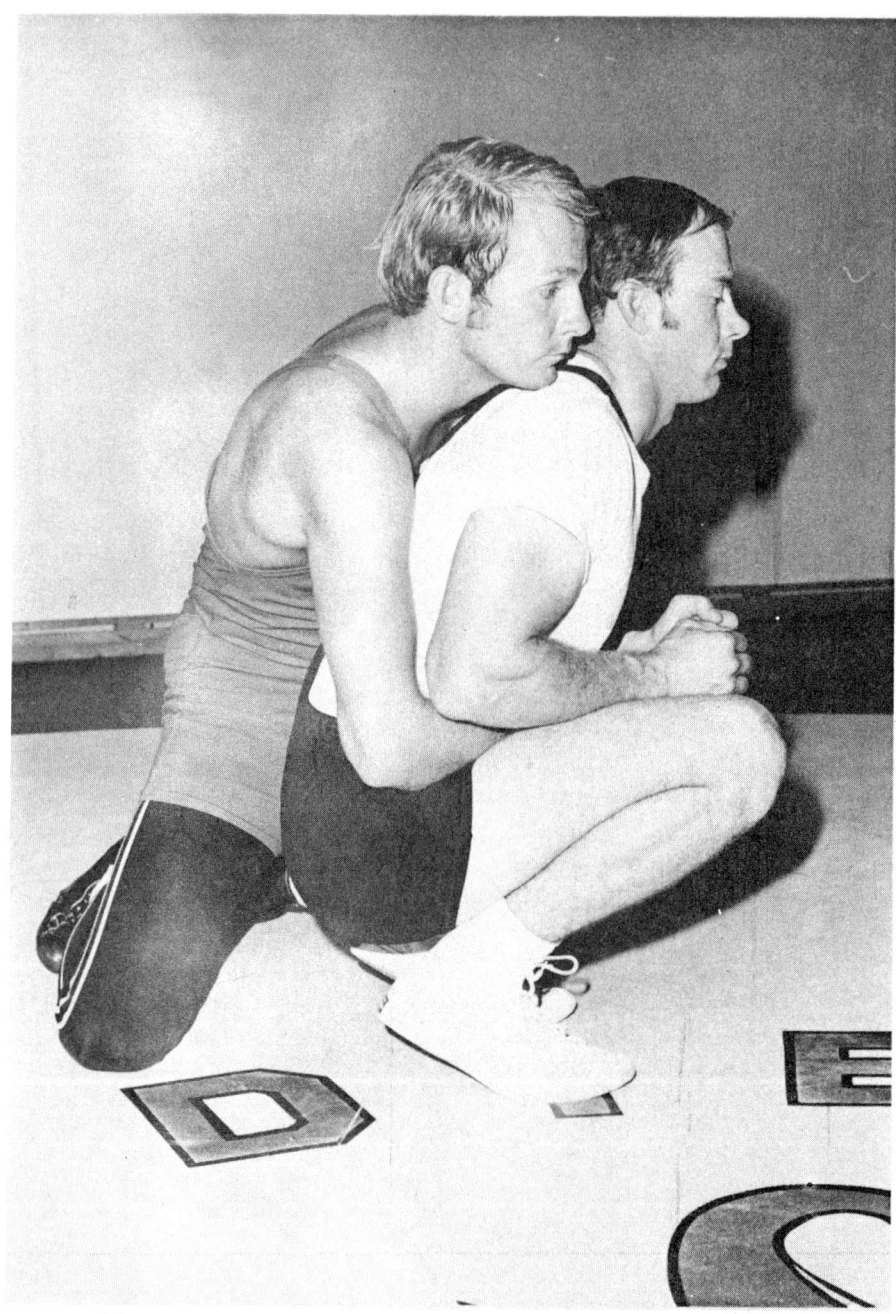

88A Bump Back Stand Up. Pushing back into opponent.

215 / STANDING CHAIN WRESTLING

88B Squatting with the weight resting on the toes, the back straight, and the elbows held in close to the body.

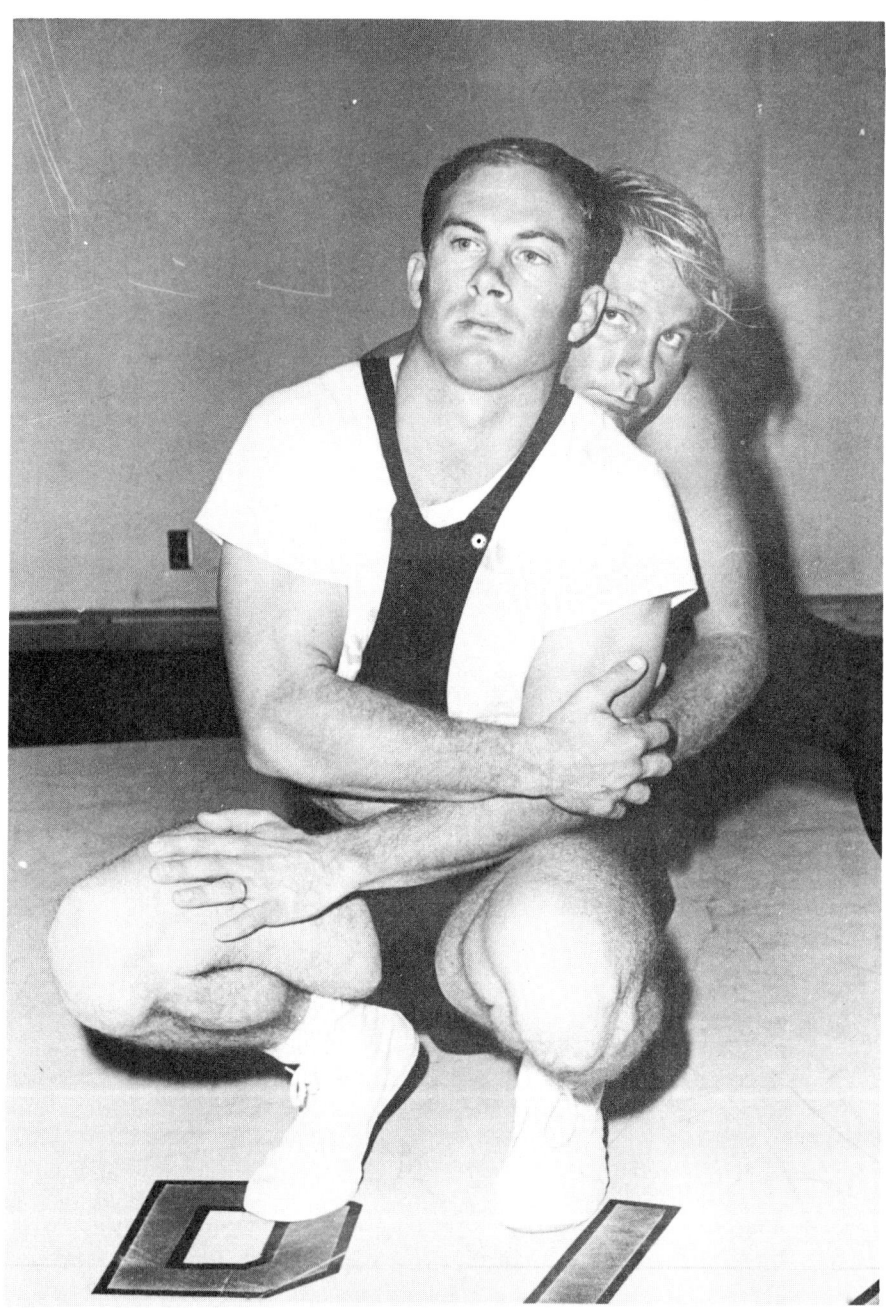

88C   Grasping opponent's hands located at the elbow.

217 / STANDING CHAIN WRESTLING

88D Obtaining a hold of the hand that is around the waist after forcing opponent's other hand behind the body.

88E Moving out to the side while turning to face opponent.

A few of the better counters to stand-ups that can be used in standing chain wrestling are as follows:

89A Near Leg Lift. Grasping opponent's ankle and lifting his leg onto the raised thigh.

219 / STANDING CHAIN WRESTLING

89B Reaching down under the thigh and locking the hands.

89C Lifting the leg with locked grip while maintaining pressure with the forearm as a means of turning him onto his back.

90A Tree Top. Picking up bottom man's leg as he stands up.

221 / STANDING CHAIN WRESTLING

90B Continuing to raise the leg thus upsetting his balance.

90C Controlling the leg while forcing him to the mat.

91A Leg Sweep. Picking up bottom man's leg as he stands up.

91B Tripping him forward by sweeping his leg and driving a shoulder into his thigh.

225 / STANDING CHAIN WRESTLING

91C Retaining control of the leg while moving into him.

Some of the most effective escape and reversal techniques that can be employed in standing chain wrestling are presented below.

92A Standing Switch. Faking to one side causing opponent to react by moving in the opposite direction.

227 / STANDING CHAIN WRESTLING

92B Reaching back between opponent's legs while grasping his hand.

92C Sitting down.

92D Turning to a position of top.

93A Standing Cross Arm Roll. Grasping opponent's wrist as he pushes forward.

SYSTEMATIC CHAMPIONSHIP WRESTLING / 230

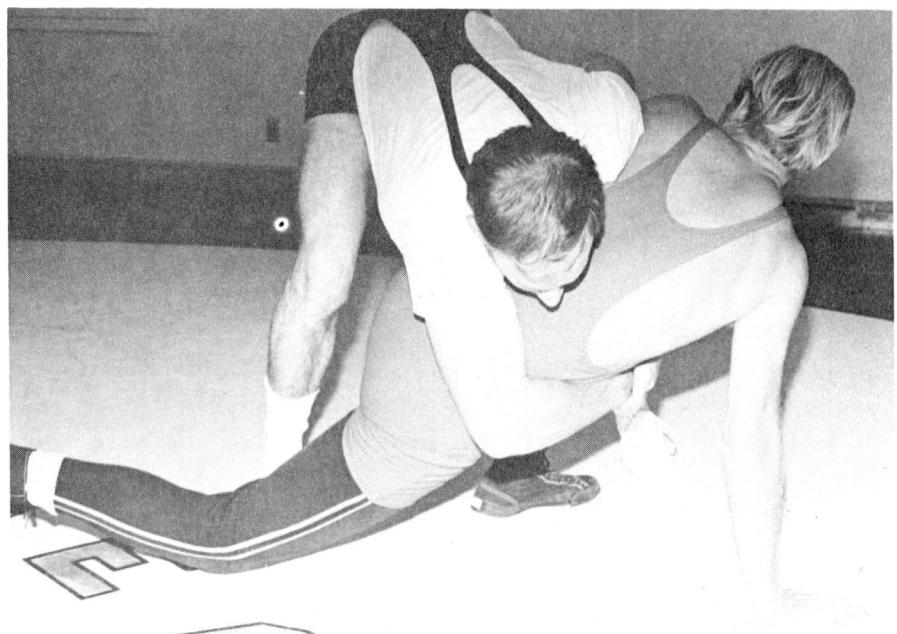

93B   Posting one hand while blocking the opponent's rear leg.

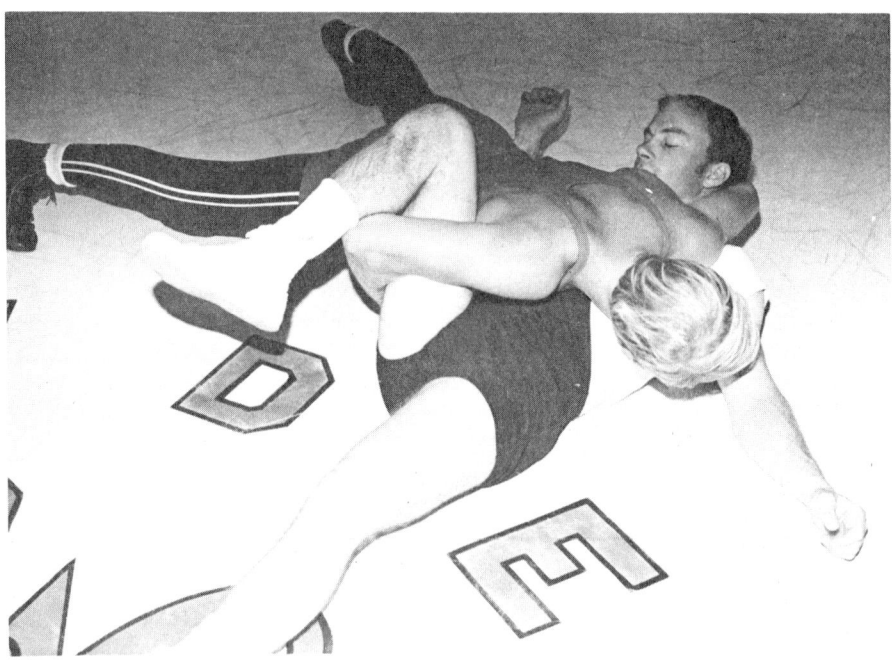

93C   Turning toward opponent's legs after coming down on top of him.

94A Back Breaker. Pulling up on opponent's arms while bending the knees.

94B Stepping behind and hooking his legs.

94C Lifting opponent off the mat and gently lowering him while maintaining a hold of his legs.

The following are counters employed from a rear standing posture.

95A Panther Whirl. Following the bottom man up to a standing position.

235 / STANDING CHAIN WRESTLING

95B Striking the back of opponent's heel while turning and falling backward.

96A Forward Trip. Wrapping a leg around one of opponent's legs and driving into him.

237 / STANDING CHAIN WRESTLING

96B Tripping opponent forward by sweeping his leg back and pushing into him with the chest and shoulder.

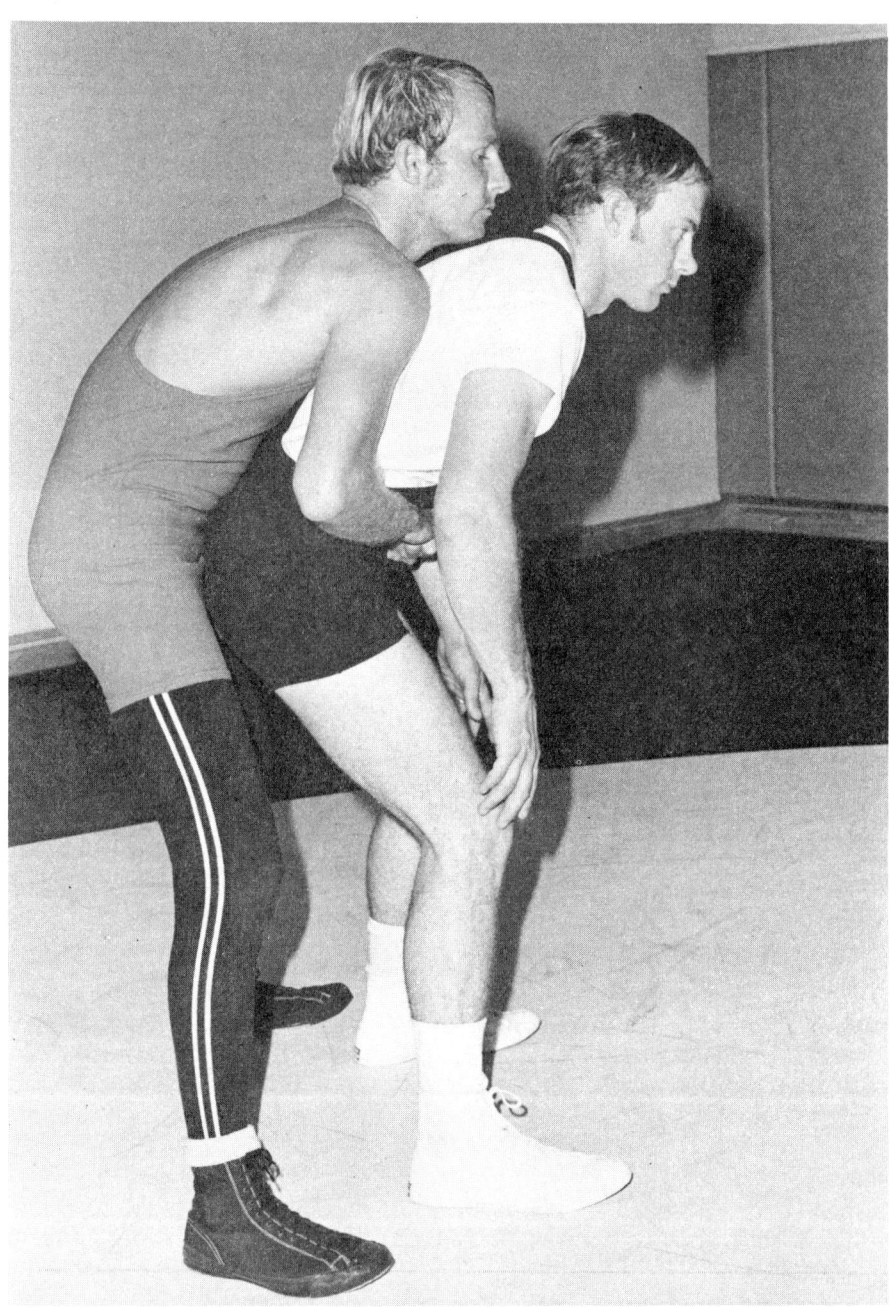

97A Tilt. Gripping opponent tightly around the waist.

97B Lifting and tilting opponent to one side.

97C Moving up on opponent's body upon making contact with the mat.

In the referee's position, the wrestler should have some sort of plan of action in mind. This plan must entail more than just one move. The possibilities of other moves, rather than just one move alone, must be given consideration. In other words, the wrestler's thoughts must be on an overall pattern of possibilities. He must be ready to select from several techniques that might be appropriate relative to an opponent's most likely reaction to block or counter his initial attempt to escape.

Chain wrestling requires that variations of particular holds be considered and taught together. When learned in sequence, these holds are more likely to be successful than if learned individually.

The best method of teaching chain wrestling is to select a limited number of moves and organize them into series drills. These drills should be continuous in nature and conducted in a noncompetitive manner. Their primary purpose is to develop a wrestler's skill in executing moves in a continuous, uninterrupted series. Emphasis should be upon constant movement. Attention should be focused on being alert to weaknesses in the opponent's position.

Until a reasonable degree of proficiency is attained, these drills should incorporate only a limited number of techniques. As the wrestler becomes more familiar with a particular series, additional techniques can be added. Once the general pattern is mastered, more details concerning the effective execution of the drill can be introduced.

Most drills begin with the wrestlers starting in the referee's position. The simplest procedure is to designate the offensive wrestler as "A" and the defensive wrestler as "B." Instruction should then be given on the sequence of moves. This sequence must be logical. When first introduced, it should be kept simple with each wrestler having to perform only one or two moves. Then, as familiarity with the drill increases, additional techniques should be added.

The number of combinations is astronomical. It is dependent only upon the imagination and ingenuity of the coach. Examples of chain drills which employ techniques discussed and illustrated in this book are as follows:

Example #1
"A" does an inside leg stand up;
"B" counters with a panther whirl;
"A" performs an outside leg stand up;
"A" completes the series with a standing switch.

Example #2
"A" executes an outside leg stand up;
"B" counters with a tilt;
"A" uses a bump back stand up;
"A" follows up with a back breaker.

Example #3
"A" performs a bump back stand up;
"B" counters with a forward trip;
"A" does an inside leg stand up;
"A" completes the series with a standing cross arm roll.

The drills should be performed rapidly. As soon as the series has been completed the wrestlers should be expected to return, without delay, to the referee's position.

Chain drills aid in the recognition and anticipation of situations where an opponent is vulnerable. This vulnerability occurs most frequently when the opponent is given very little time to adjust to changing circumstances. Time lapses for contemplating a new set of circumstances can be kept to a minimum when several moves are performed in a series. Learning to perform moves in series is best achieved through chain wrestling drills.

28
Freeing the Hands

THE PROPER EXECUTION OF MOST WRESTLING TECHNIQUES REQUIRES THE ability to free the hands. Rarely, however, does this elementary phase of wrestling receive adequate attention. Learning it is often taken for granted. This causes it to be performed haphazardly.

Failure to devote sufficient time to learning how to efficiently free the hands results in a wasteful expenditure of energy. By eliminating unnecessary movements, the level of performance can be improved and the consumption of energy decreased.

Expenditure of energy is directly related to the efficiency at which a skill is performed. It is the ratio of the amount of work accomplished to the amount of energy expended. The smaller the expenditure the greater the efficiency.

Most wrestling techniques by themselves are easily countered. It is only when they are combined with certain fundamental skills that they become truly effective.

The application of fundamentals in combination with wrestling techniques vastly improves the chances of these techniques being successful. How successful depends upon how well the fundamentals are learned. They are the prerequisites to success.

Fundamentals are a necessary part of skilled performance. Only when they are taught early and practiced continually throughout the season will they be mastered. Sufficient time must be devoted to teaching them if they are to be effectively employed.

Teaching should start with basic fundamentals. These fundamentals should become the building blocks upon which more advanced movement patterns are built. Without them, even the most effective wrestling technique will often fail.

243 / FREEING THE HANDS

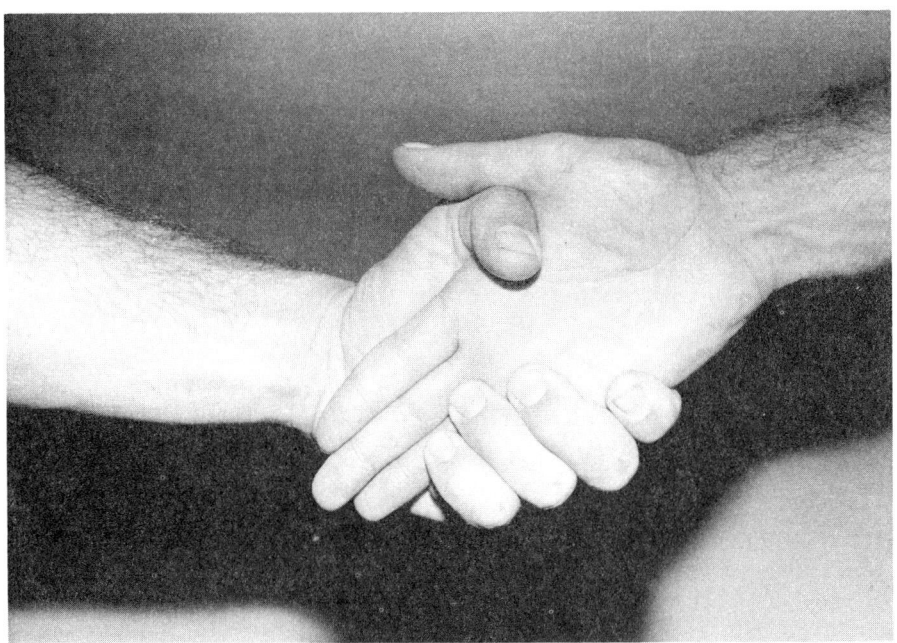

98A   Situation #1. Having the fingers of one hand controlled.

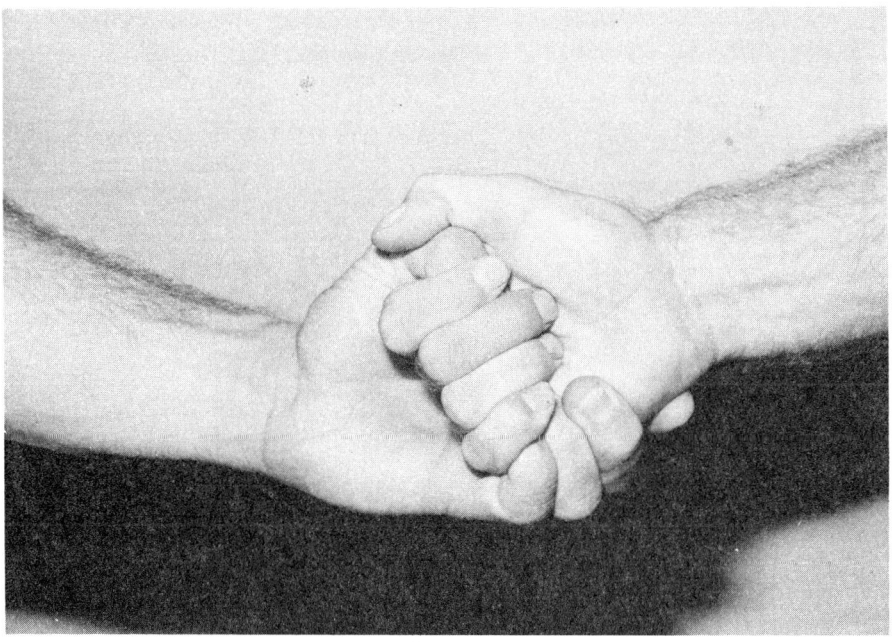

98B   Eliminating opponent's advantage by flexing the fingers and applying an identical grip to his fingers.

SYSTEMATIC CHAMPIONSHIP WRESTLING / 244

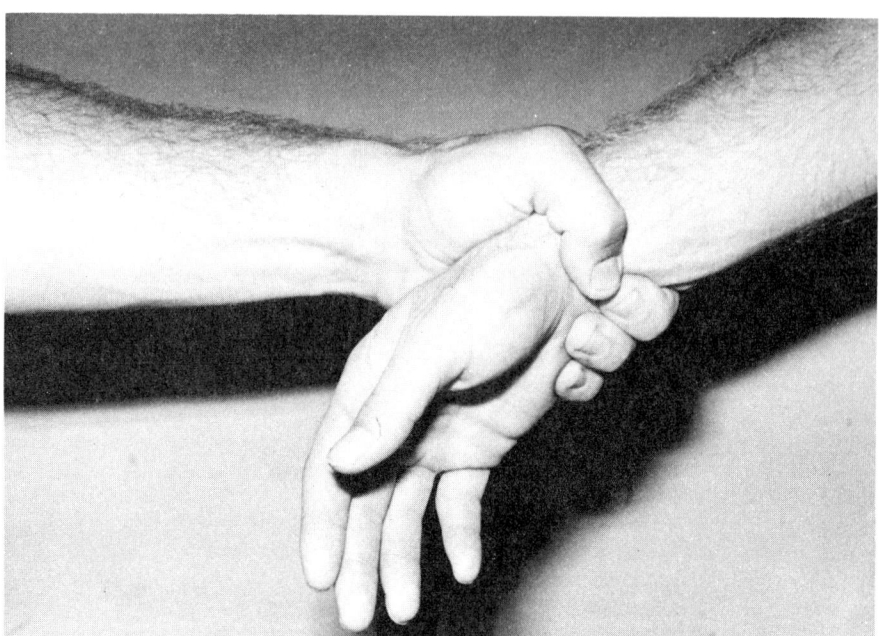

99A Situation #2. Having the opponent grasp the wrist instead of the fingers.

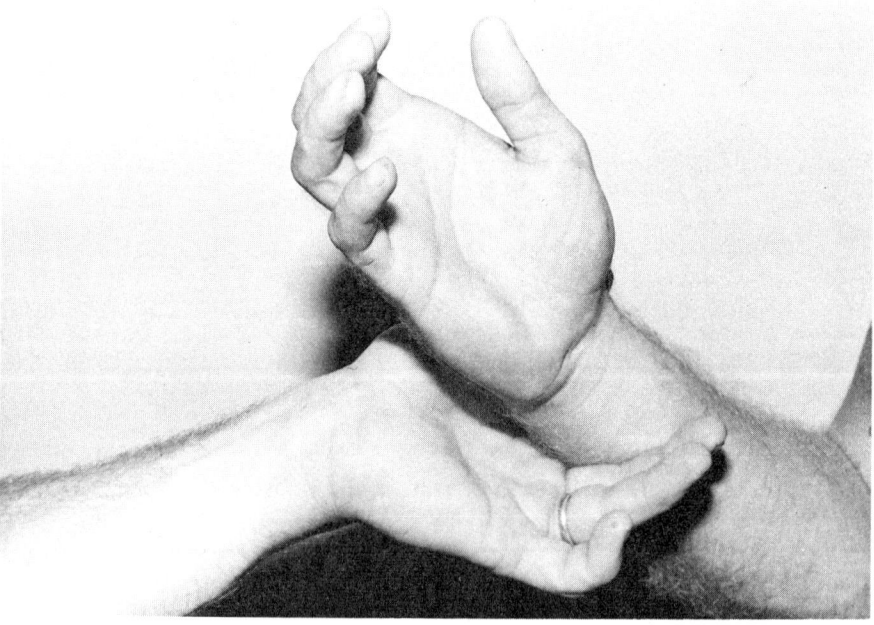

99B Freeing the captured wrist by straightening and rotating the hand in a circular fashion while lifting up against the opponent's thumb.

245 / FREEING THE HANDS

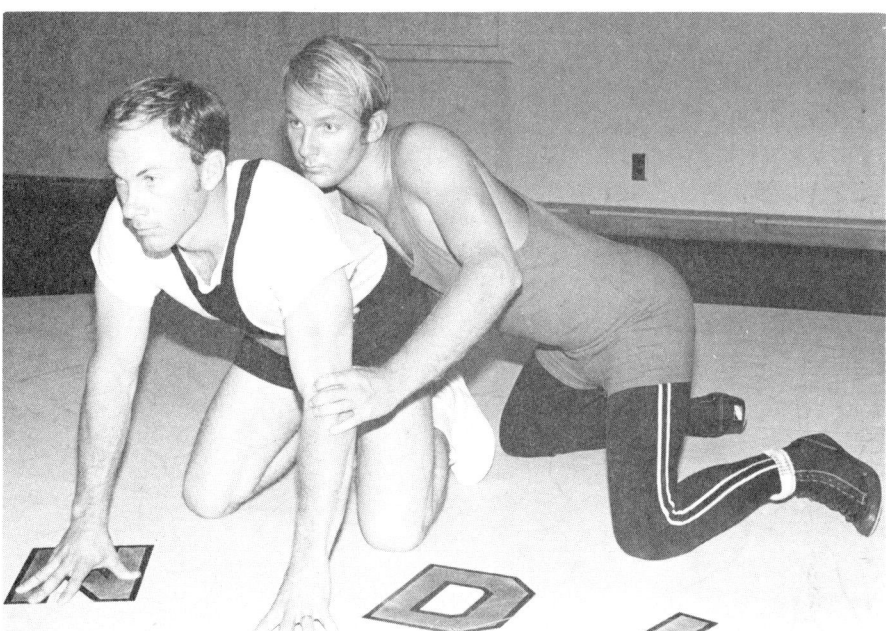

100A Situation #3. Having the inside arm controlled by opponent in the referee's position.

100B Striking the edge of opponent's hand.

101A Situation #4. Having a wrist grasped from the inside.

247 / FREEING THE HANDS

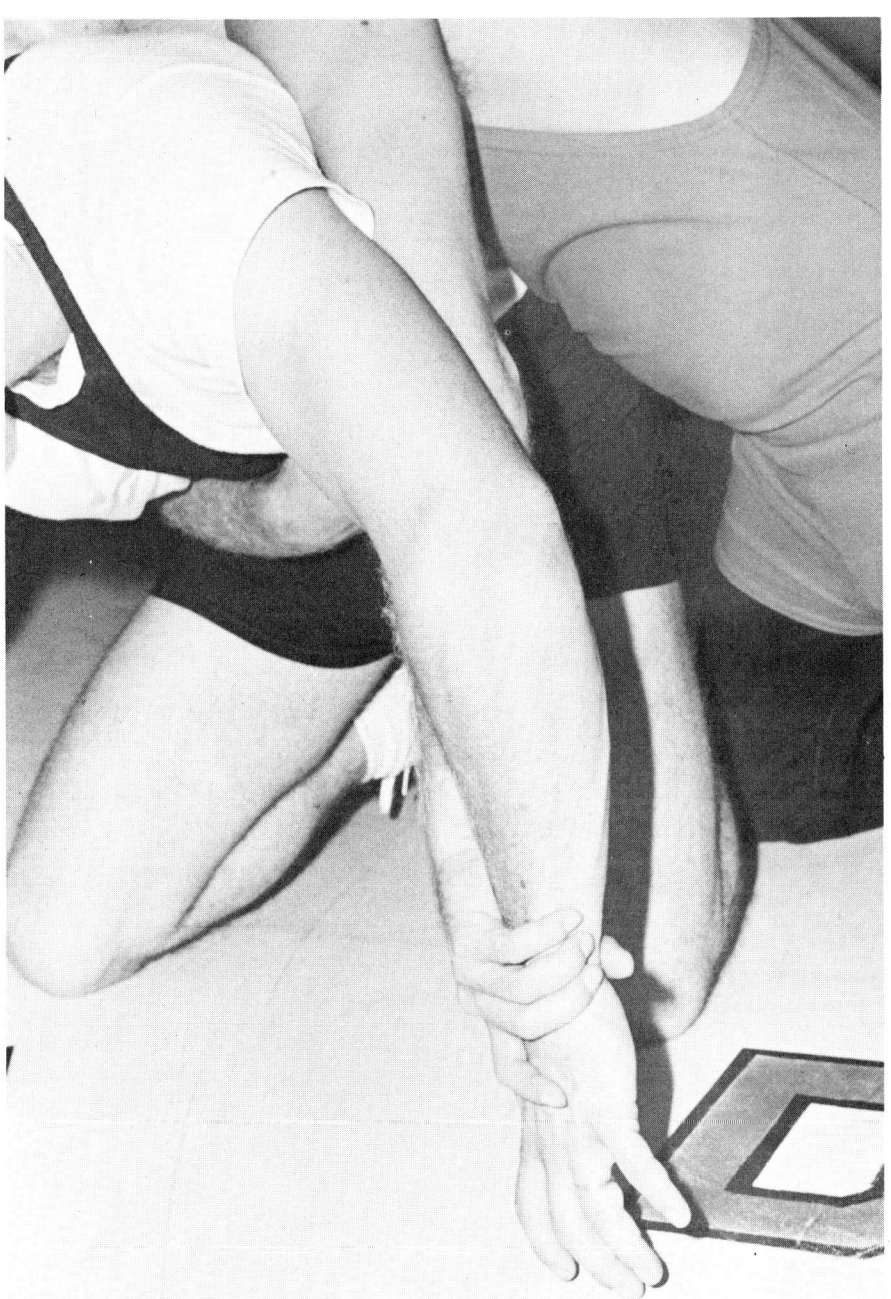

101B Breaking the hold by rotating the wrist out and away from the body.

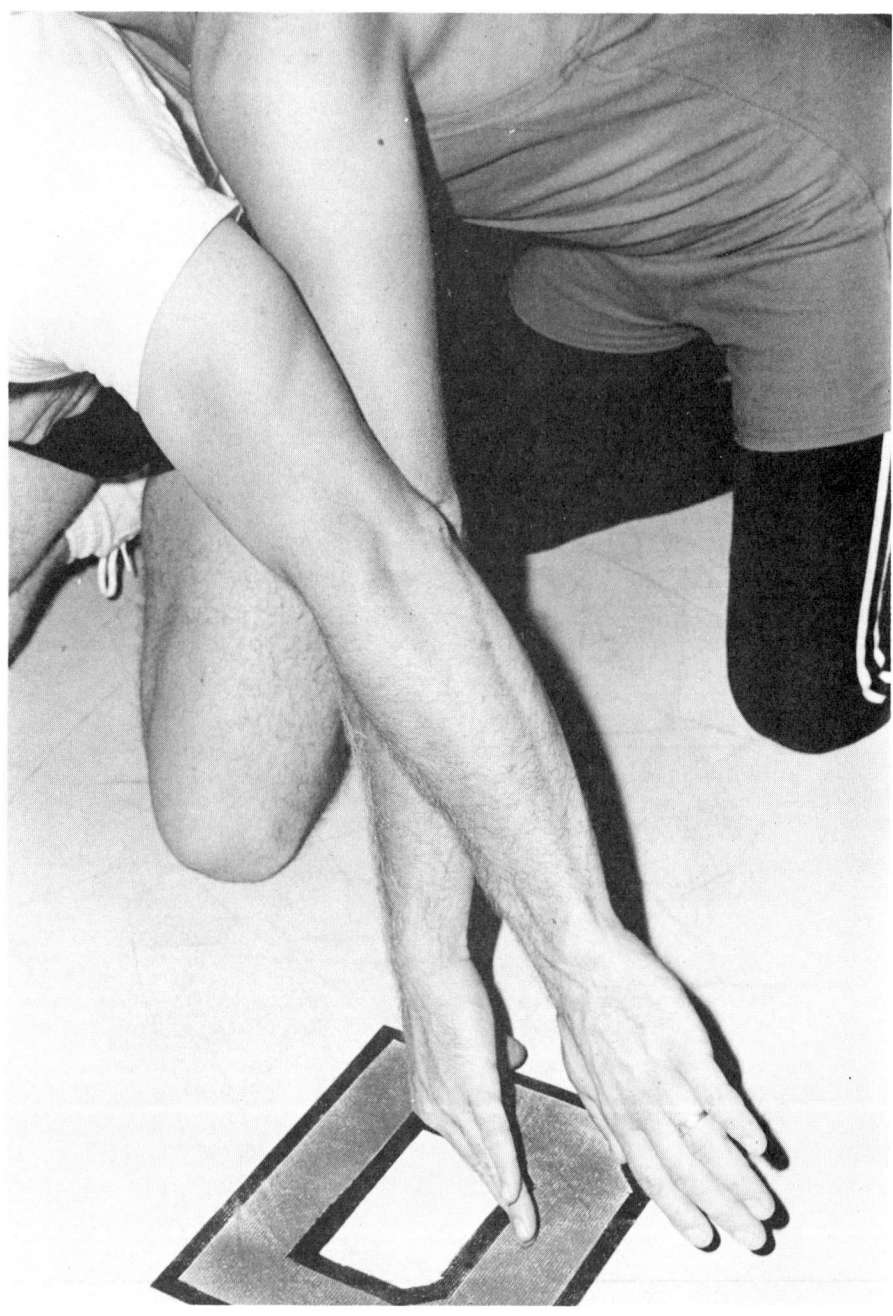

101C Continuing to extend the arm to gain leverage in freeing the wrist.

249 / FREEING THE HANDS

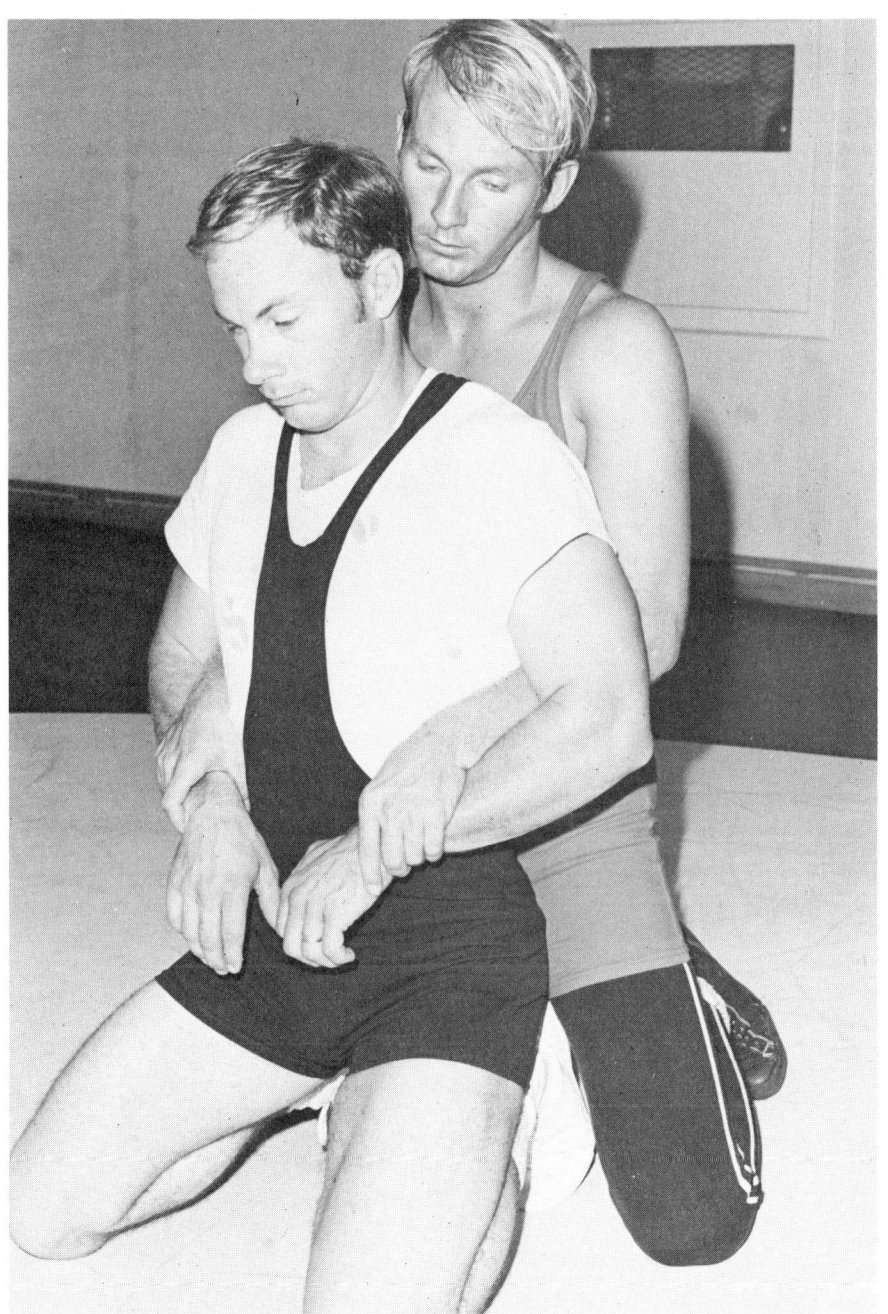

102A Situation #5. Having opponent grasp both wrists.

102B Rotating the wrists down and outward.

251 / FREEING THE HANDS

102C Extending the arms away from the body to free the wrists.

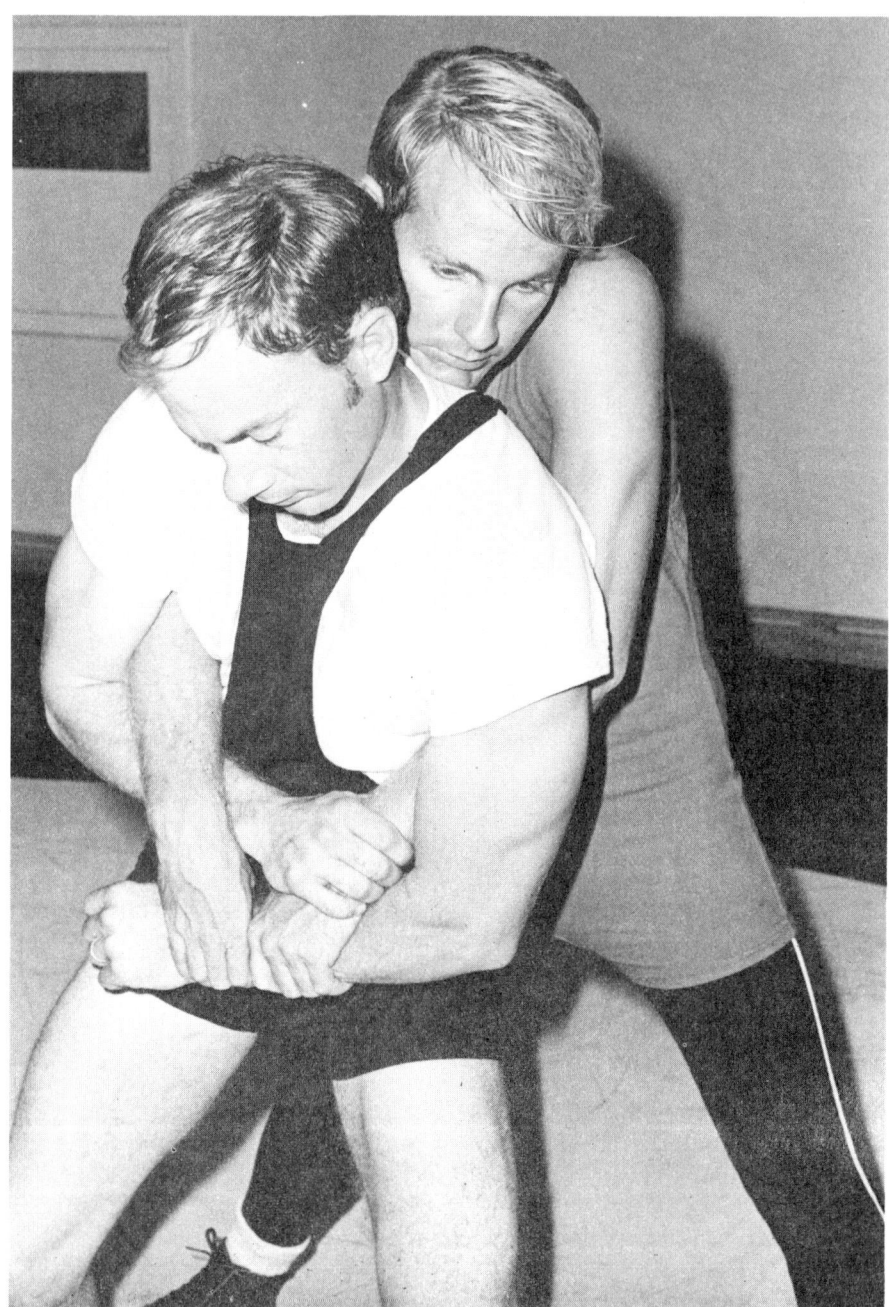

103A Situation #6. Breaking the two-on-one bar arm hold by reaching behind opponent's arm, grasping the wrist of the captured arm, and prying upward.

253 / FREEING THE HANDS

103B Rotating the arms down and outward to free them.

29
The Seven Most Effective Escape and Reversal Techniques Employed by N.C.A.A. Champions*

A PROBLEM COMMONLY FACED BY WRESTLING COACHES IS THAT OF SELECTing and teaching those escape and reversal techniques which will do the most to complement their efforts to produce winning teams. The common practice has been for coaches to teach those techniques which in their opinions, based on past experiences, have been most effective for them. Generally, however, coaches who have suggested one technique was superior to another had little bases for such a claim other than personal observation and experience, since there was a paucity of published scientific or experimental evidence to support any such conclusion. With this in mind, it was the intention of the author to provide some sort of scientific bases for agreement as to which techniques are actually most effective.

In order to achieve this objective, the author researched escape and reversal techniques employed in the National Collegiate Athletic Association championship wrestling matches over a period of sixteen years. Using an analysis of the escape and reversal techniques employed by this large sample of top-flight wrestlers in top-flight competition, an index to the relative effectiveness of each technique was established. Only those techniques which were attempted over a minimum of fifty times are included in this summary. The resulting index is valuable in differentiating between the effectiveness of the various techniques. It also provides a scientific foundation upon which coaches can base their opinions as to which techniques are truly most effective. The word "effective," as it is used in this summary, refers to those techniques which can be employed with the greatest possibility of being

---

* This article reprinted with the permission of *Scholastic Wrestling News*, October 23, 1970.

255 / TECHNIQUES EMPLOYED BY N.C.A.A. CHAMPIONS

successful while extending the greatest assurance that if countered they will not result in losing points for the wrestler attempting them.

Critical analysis was selected as the method of research since it best reveals what actually occurs in performance. It quantifies the qualitative aspects of performance. It is a very practical method of research since it can be used to determine the extent to which a technique has a direct and immediate effect upon the winning or losing of an event.

There are four phases to analysis: (1) observing, (2) recording, (3) categorizing, and (4) interpreting. Observing was done when the author viewed sixteen years of films of the N.C.A.A. championship wrestling matches. The recording and categorizing was done by use of the following score card. It was possible, through the use of this card, to check the number of times a particular technique was employed in gaining points, losing points, or neither gaining nor losing points for the wrestler attempting the technique.

SCORE CARD FOR RECORDING DATA

Escape or Reversal Technique	Points Gained	Number Points Gained or Lost	Points Lost

All attempted escape and reversal techniques occurring during the observations were recorded in one of three categories. Each of the categories was kept exclusive, and therefore, each of the attempted techniques fit into one and only one of the categories. After each technique was identified and recorded, a careful recheck was made which indicated a high degree of accuracy. Recording involved classification of each attempted technique into one of three categories: (1) attempts that gained points, (2) attempts that lost points, and (3) attempts that neither gained nor lost points. A total of 1447 attempts was included in these categories. Responses in categories 1 and 2 affected the scores of the matches, whereas responses in category 3 obviously did not. A summary of these categorized responses for the seven most effective techniques is as follows:

TABLE 5
Score Card With Raw Data

Escape or Reversal Technique	Category #1 No. Attempts Resulting In Points Gained	Category #2 No. Attempts Resulting In Points Lost	Category #3 No. Attempts Resulting In No Points Gained Or Lost
Sit-out	66	7	101
Stand-up	179	1	412
Shoulder-roll	15	1	41
Side-roll	12	1	45
Switch	28	0	104
Whizzer	12	3	53
Stand-up-switch	11	0	56

In the 156 championship matches observed, the whizzer (photo 109A), for example, was attempted a total of 68 times. Twelve of those attempts represented a gain in points, resulting in a net increase in the chances of winning, whereas three attempts represented a loss in points, tending to lower the chances of winning. The remaining 53 attempts resulted in no change; these may be significant pedagogically, but they have no influence on the scores and, therefore, represent a waste of time and effort.

In order to make the data in Table 5 more useful from a practical standpoint, it was converted to percentiles by means of the following ratios:

$$\% \text{ of attempts resulting in points being gained} = \frac{\text{No. attempts that gained points}}{\text{No. attempts that gained points} + \text{No. attempts that no points were gained or lost} + \text{No. attempts that lost points}}$$

$$\% \text{ of attempts resulting in no points being lost} = \frac{\text{No. attempts that gained points} + \text{No. attempts that no points were gained or lost}}{\text{No. attempts that gained points} + \text{No. attempts that no points were gained or lost} + \text{No. attempts that lost points}}$$

The overall effectiveness of each technique was calculated by using the following formula:

$$\% \text{ of effectiveness} = \frac{\% \text{ of attempts resulting in points being gained} + \% \text{ of attempts resulting in no points being lost}}{2}$$

Then, using the resulting percentages, the following table was compiled:

TABLE 6

Index of the Seven Most Effective Escape and Reversal Techniques Employed by N.C.A.A. Champions*

Escape or Reversal Technique	Column "A" % of Attempts Likely to Result In Points Being Gained	Column "B" % of Attempts Likely to Result In no Points Being Lost	Column "C" % of Overall Effectiveness
Sit-out	40	95	65
Stand-up	30	100	65
Shoulder-roll	25	100	60
Side-roll	20	100	60
Switch	20	100	60
Whizzer	20	95	55
Stand-up-switch	15	100	55

* Figures rounded to nearest digit of five

Table 6 can be used as a source of reference as to the relative amount of assurance a coach can have that a particular escape or reversal technique will succeed (Column "A"), the approximate risk his wrestler will be taking if the technique is successfully countered (Column "B"), and the overall effectiveness or total influence the technique will likely have on the ultimate goal of winning (Column "C").

Column "A" of Table 6 shows the sit-out (photo 104A) to be the most successful escape and reversal technique used by national champions. It was successful 40% of the times it was attempted. In other words, four out of every ten times it was attempted it worked. It was also the second most popular technique used in the Nationals.

104A Sit-Out

The most popular technique was the stand-up (photo 105A). It was attempted more often than all the other six techniques combined. In fact, the stand-up accounted for approximately one-third of all the escapes and reversals employed during the sixteen years covered in this summary. In spite of its popularity, it was only the second most successful technique. Three out of every four times it was tried it gained points for the wrestler attempting it.

259 / TECHNIQUES EMPLOYED BY N.C.A.A. CHAMPIONS

105A Stand-Up

The shoulder roll (photo 106A) was the third most successful technique. One out of every four times it was attempted it worked. The side roll (photo 107A), the switch (photo 108), and the whizzer (photo 109A) were all equally successful. Each worked one-fifth of the times it was attempted. The seventh most successful technique was the stand-up-switch (photo 110A). It worked about once out of every ten times it was employed.

Column "B" of Table 6 indicates how much of a risk is being taken in possibly losing points when a particular technique is countered. In other words, it tells the coach how much of a chance his wrestler has of possibly losing points if he decides to attempt one of the seven techniques included in this summary. Of the seven techniques the sit-out and the whizzer are the most dangerous. In proportion to the total number of times each was attempted, they are equally risky. In contrast, the five other techniques are almost totally safe to use. There is only a very slight chance that these techniques will lose points by being successfully countered.

Column "C" of Table 6 shows the relative effectiveness of each technique. The sit-out and the stand-up are equally effective. The shoulder-roll, side-roll, and switch are the next most effective techniques. The

106A Shoulder-Roll

261 / TECHNIQUES EMPLOYED BY N.C.A.A. CHAMPIONS

107A Side-Roll

108A Switch

109A Whizzer

whizzer and stand-up-switch rank sixth and seventh in effectiveness. Although both the whizzer and the stand-up-switch are equal in effectiveness, they differ in that the whizzer is more likely to gain points for the wrestler attempting it while the stand-up-switch is less likely to lose points if it is countered.

Depending upon the circumstances, a coach may be wiser to encourage a wrestler to attempt a technique that has a higher risk factor than another. In general, however, a coach would be wisest to play the percentages and only resort to calculated risks when time is running out and his wrestler is losing.

263 / TECHNIQUES EMPLOYED BY N.C.A.A. CHAMPIONS

110A Stand-Up-Switch

30
The Long Versus the Short Sit-Out

THERE ARE TWO TYPES OF WRESTLING SIT-OUTS; THE LONG AND THE SHORT. Both are initiated from the referee's position by planting the sole of one foot on the mat while shooting the other forward. Both commonly employ a sudden turning of the body to the left or right at the completion of movement pattern.

Executing the long sit out properly requires that the inside leg be swung out as far as possible while the body is extended to its fullest length.

In order to be effective, the long sit-out must be performed with considerable speed. It oftentimes will have to be repeated several times in rapid succession before being successful. Having to repeat it continually requires the expenditure of a considerable amount of energy and therefore often discourages its use. It is mainly effective when employed against a lazy or fatigued opponent who is slow in initiating a counter.

The most common counter for the long sit out is executed by hooking a hand under the armpit, dragging and moving behind. It is about the only one generally used to counter a long sit-out. The counter will not gain points for the wrestler employing it, but it does make it possible for him to maintain his position of advantage. The long sit-out, basically, is not a dangerous technique since it cannot lose points for the wrestler attempting it when it is countered.

In contrast to the long sit-out, which is designed only as an escape, the short sit-out can be employed as either an escape or a reversal.

The short sit-out requires the wrestler employing it to assume a sitting position on his buttocks with the elbows generally tight to the sides of the body and the back and legs slightly bent.

In order for the short sit-out to be effective, the opponent must make the mistake of either positioning his head or an arm over one of the bottom man's shoulders. Once this mistake is made, it can immediately be capitalized upon. Depending upon whether the mistake was

265 / LONG VERSUS THE SHORT SIT-OUT

111A Long Sit Out. Planting the sole of one foot on the mat.

111B Shooting the rear leg forward.

111C Assuming an elongated sitting position prior to turning.

112A Short Sit Out. Planting the sole of one foot on the mat.

267 / LONG VERSUS THE SHORT SIT-OUT

112B Shooting the rear leg forward.

112C Assuming a sitting position prior to turning.

SYSTEMATIC CHAMPIONSHIP WRESTLING / 268

113A Over Drag Counter to Long Sit Out. Maintaining a position behind the bottom man who initiates a long sit out by stepping forward with the outside foot.

113B Preparing to counter while opponent shoots his leg through as far as possible and drops to his side.

269 / LONG VERSUS THE SHORT SIT-OUT

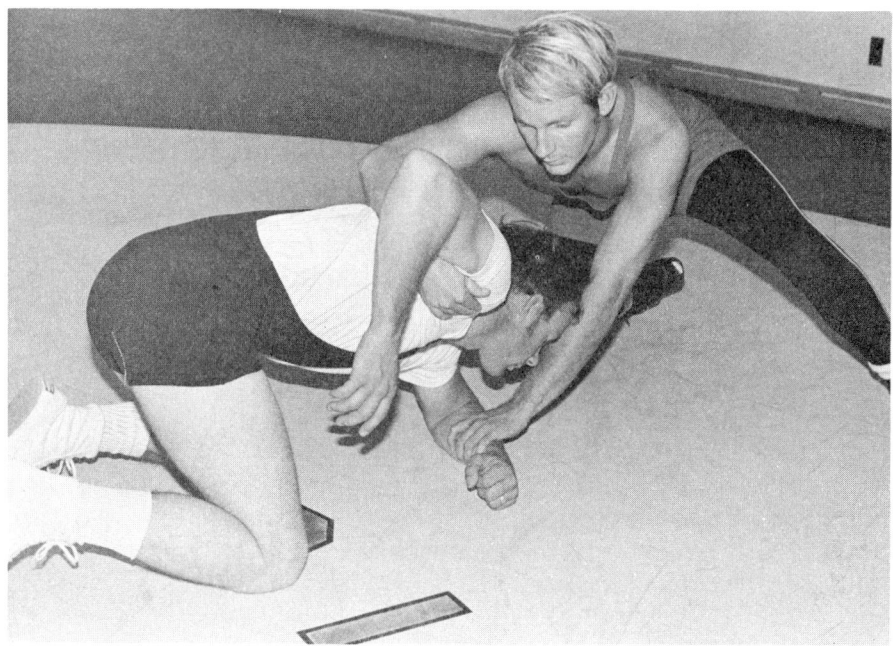

113C   Reaching across to overhook an arm as the bottom man pivots on his elbow.

113D   Pulling and spinning in the opposite direction of the bottom man's sit out.

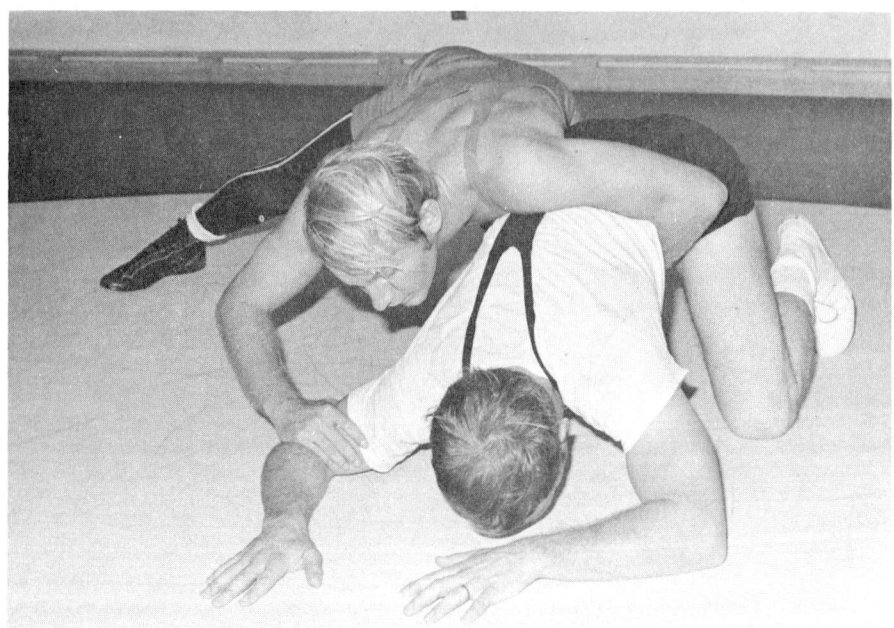

113E   Spinning to a position behind.

in positioning the head or arm will largely determine which maneuver will be used from the sitting position.

Unlike the long sit-out, the short sit-out is a very risky technique. Due to the precarious sitting position that must be assumed in executing the short sit-out, it is possible for the wrestler attempting it to lose points or be pinned if it is successfully countered. While sitting on his buttocks, he is in a very unstable position. His balance is easily upset when he is pulled backwards. Once his balance has been upset, he encounters great difficulty in returning to his original sitting position. While sitting, he has very limited mobility and is quite vulnerable to the rear where there is little support.

In conclusion, the long sit-out can be said to be more tiring to employ, more limited in possible variations, and more easily countered. The short sit-out, on the other hand, has more options, is more dependent upon the opponent making a mistake to be successful, has more ways of being countered, and is more risky in terms of losing points for the wrestler attempting it when it is successfully countered.

114A Sit Out and Head Pull. Grasping opponent's head when it is placed over one of the defensive man's shoulders.

114B Dropping to one shoulder.

114C Turning, thus forcing the top man over onto the mat.

273 / LONG VERSUS THE SHORT SIT-OUT

114D   Moving immediately into a pinning combination.

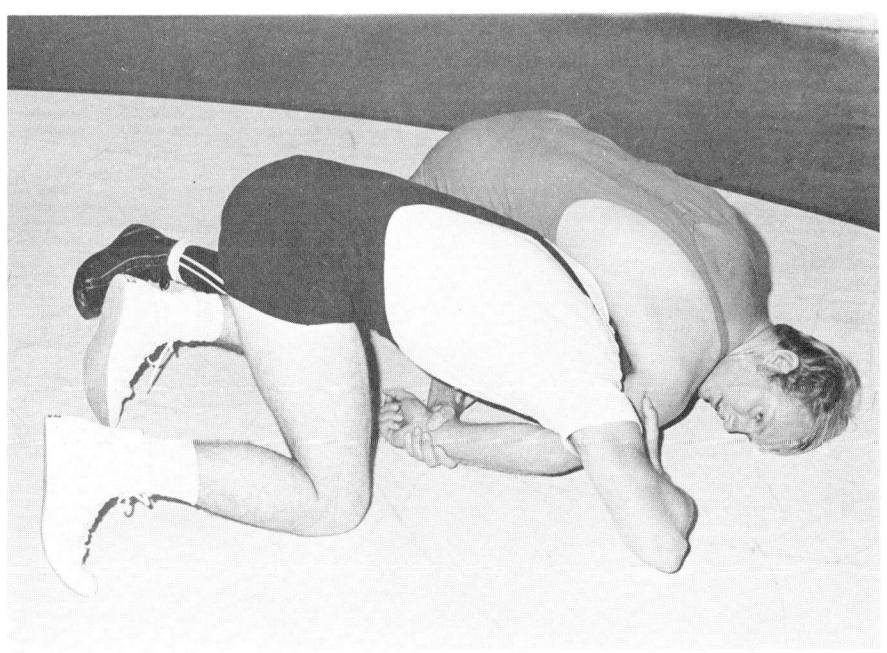

115A   Sit Out and Arm Pull. Grasping the offensive man's arm when it is placed over a shoulder.

SYSTEMATIC CHAMPIONSHIP WRESTLING / 274

115B Starting to turn by dropping to his shoulder.

115C Continuing to turn while whipping the arm under opponent's arm.

275 / LONG VERSUS THE SHORT SIT-OUT

115D Recovering to a riding position.

116A Drop Back Counter to Short Sit Out. Being careful not to lean forward with the head when the bottom man begins to sit out.

SYSTEMATIC CHAMPIONSHIP WRESTLING / 276

116B   Moving out to a slight angle while pulling down on the bottom man's shoulders.

116C   Grasping the chin and pulling the opponent back sharply into a pinning combination.

277 / LONG VERSUS THE SHORT SIT-OUT

117A Cradle Counter to Short Sit Out. Reaching around the bottom man's neck with one arm and under his knee with the other.

117B Lifting up on the knee and locking the hands.

SYSTEMATIC CHAMPIONSHIP WRESTLING / 278

117C Dropping back to the mat and overhooking the free leg.

118A Spin Counter to Short Sit Out. Applying pressure to the bottom man's back in order to get him to lower his head.

279 / LONG VERSUS THE SHORT SIT-OUT

118B Beginning to spin around to the front.

118C Securing the bottom man's head under an armpit while lifting on his knees to force his back to the mat.

119A Cross Face Counter to Short Sit Out. Reaching over and grasping the bottom man's upper arm while bringing the other hand under his leg.

119B Scooting out to the side, hooking the leg, locking hands, and dropping the bottom man back to the mat.

31
Unusual Standing Escapes and Reversals

SOME LESS COMMONLY ATTEMPTED ESCAPES AND REVERSALS CAN BE MORE effective than some popular ones. The most effective techniques are those which gain points the major portion of the times they are attempted and rarely lose points when they are countered.

The escapes and reversals discussed in this chapter are somewhat less common than most. Consequently, they are less likely to be expected. They are more likely to succeed since the opponent will probably not have practiced a defense or counter to them.

These escapes and reversals are not so risky as many others, simply because they are employed from standing. While standing, the wrestler is harder to control and more difficult to score points against than in any other position.

If while in a rear standing position the opponent has either of his legs located between the defensive man's legs, he can be reversed (photos 120A through 120C). By reaching down and grasping his ankle with both hands, it can be lifted off the mat. He may then be forced to the mat if the wrestler continues to lift the leg while simultaneously sitting back. Once on the mat, a cradle pinning combination can be applied.

If an opponent positions his head over the defensive man's shoulder, he can be reversed (photos 121A through 121C). The nape of the neck is grasped and pulled forward. Then, by stepping through and securing a hold on the leg, he can be forced to the mat.

Anytime an opponent positions his arm over one of the defensive wrestler's arms, he can be reversed (photos 122A through 122C). The technique is initiated by grasping the opponent's arm and simultaneously dropping down to one knee. The captured arm is forced upward and a quick turn completes the technique.

120A Between the Legs Pick Up. Reaching down and picking up one of opponent's legs.

283 / UNUSUAL STANDING ESCAPES AND REVERSALS

120B Lifting the leg and sitting back into opponent.

120C Applying a cradle pin.

121A Head Pull. Reaching back and grasping opponent's head.

285 / UNUSUAL STANDING ESCAPES AND REVERSALS

121B Turning, stepping through, and grasping opponent's leg.

121C Forcing opponent to the mat and securing a pinning combination.

122A Arm Pull. Being controlled with a hold that encircles one of the arms.

122B Driving the trapped arm upward while dropping down to one knee.

289 / UNUSUAL STANDING ESCAPES AND REVERSALS

122C Turning in and recovering to a riding position.

To obtain a double wrist lock (photos 123A through 123B), one arm should be placed over the opponent's elbow as high as possible. The other hand is then used to reach through and grasp the wrist of the first arm. By exerting force in a perpendicular direction to the long axis of the opponent's body, an escape is realized. Caution must be exercised not to apply force in the direction of the opponent's head.

An opponent, who positions the top of his head in the small of the defensive man's back, can be reversed (photos 124A and 124B). The opponent's hands should be grasped and held firmly. Then by bending backward, weight can be placed over the nape of his neck. A stepping motion forward combined with an arched back will force him down to a prone position on the mat. A quick turn toward his legs will assure at least an escape.

If an opponent stands close with a loose hold around the waist, he can be reversed (photos 125A through 125D). It is begun by placing the palms of both hands under the interlocked hands of the opponent. The knees are suddenly collapsed. This lowers the body weight while forcing the opponent's arms upward.

123A Double Wristlock. Controlling the offensive man by grasping the wrist after placing it over one of opponent's arms.

291 / UNUSUAL STANDING ESCAPES AND REVERSALS

123B Applying pressure perpendicular to opponent's body in achieving an escape.

124A Walk Out. Having the top of the offensive man's head in the small of the back.

293 / UNUSUAL STANDING ESCAPES AND REVERSALS

124B Arching the back and placing weight over the offensive's man's head while securing a grip on his locked hands.

125A Back Breaker. Pulling opponent's locked arms up and under the armpits.

295 / UNUSUAL STANDING ESCAPES AND REVERSALS

125B Lowering the body weight by bending the knees.

125C Stepping behind one of opponent's legs.

297 / UNUSUAL STANDING ESCAPES AND REVERSALS

125D Hooking both arms around opponent's legs, lifting him off the mat, and gently lowering him while maintaining a hold of his legs.

Forcing the arms up under the armpits allows the hips to be moved freely. A step is then taken behind the opponent. The arms are hooked behind his legs. There is little he can do to prevent himself from being lifted off the mat. He is then lowered to the mat.

The defensive wrestler, while in the position of disadvantage, has to use an escape or reversal in order to gain points toward winning the match. In accomplishing this goal, he has the option of employing several techniques. It is oftentimes more advantageous to attempt an unusual standing escape or reversal. Such techniques involve the least risk of losing points if countered while possessing the element of surprise.

Part VI
RIDES TO PINNING COMBINATIONS

32
Wrestle to Win

WRESTLING IS A PERCENTAGE GAME—A GAME WHERE THE VAST MAJORITY of matches are won on points rather than pins. Playing this game according to the percentages means gambling only when the odds are overwhelmingly in one's favor or a situation warrants a calculated risk. Strategy requires that the wrestler do nothing to jeopardize his chances of winning and that he resort to gambling only as a last resort.

In the author's opinion, emphasis in any wrestling program should be upon takedowns and escapes. Riding techniques should be of secondary consideration. A wrestler who can take down an opponent and escape from him should be able to beat him. In other words, a wrestler does not have to be able to ride an opponent to beat him. As a matter of fact, the author suggests releasing an opponent who is difficult to control rather than risking the loss of two points and ending up on the bottom by trying to control him. This philosophy does the most to complement the major objective of winning.

Winning is best accomplished by wearing an opponent down. If the wrestler on top can make his opponent work harder trying to escape than he himself has to work to maintain control, he will win.

An opponent can be tired by being forced to carry and fight the additional burden of the top man's weight. While making him support his weight, the top man should remain as relaxed as possible, being careful not to exert any more force than is necessary to maintain the position of advantage.

In order to keep as much weight as possible on an opponent, the offensive wrestler should never let his uniform touch the mat. Most of his weight is over the opponent when he stays off his knees and moves about on his feet. This increases his mobility and enables him to shift positions with the least amount of effort.

Riding, basically, consists of maintaining control. Control is maintained by employing a ride that will do the most to immobilize the opponent. A mobile opponent is dangerous.

There are three basic reasons why employing rides, which tie-up an opponent's leg, do more to immobilize him than those which emphasize controlling any other part of his anatomy. Most wrestlers experience difficulty in initiating an escape or reversal without first having secured a hold on the top man's head or arm. By riding back on his legs, he has nothing to grab hold of.

The second advantage of riding a leg is that it limits the types of escapes and reversals an opponent can initiate. He is likely to be dependent upon having his legs free before attempting to escape. Unless he can free his legs, he is forced to attempt escape and reversal techniques from an all-fours position on the mat. Techniques attempted, while down on the mat, have a greater chance of losing points by being countered than they would if attempted from standing. The closer a mistake is made to the surface of the mat, the greater are the chances it will lose points for the wrestler attempting it.

The higher up on an opponent's body a ride is employed, the easier it is for him to raise to a standing position. If he gains a standing position, he has two distinct advantages not possessed while down on all fours. First, his maneuverability is extended far beyond what it would be in any other position. This increased mobility makes him harder to control.

The other advantage of the standing position is that he has only his own weight to carry around. This permits him to move faster. The weight of the top man would otherwise slow him down considerably. Also, by not having the burden of this extra weight, he is less likely to tire as quickly.

The third reason for riding an opponent's legs instead of further up on his body, is the security it offers. While controlling an opponent's legs, he is less likely to successfully gain a reversal, two points, and the position of advantage. Any time difficulty is encountered while riding an opponent's leg, the leg can be released, thus allowing the opponent to escape. The most the opponent can hope for is an escape. If, however, a ride were applied to the upper half of his opponent's body, it is possible for him to employ a switch, roll, or whizzer by anchoring the arm that is around his waist.

Wrestlers should be encouraged to ride in a manner that will keep them out of trouble. They should be coached to ride so that it is possible to turn loose of anything they have a hold on. They should be discouraged from favoring rides which place them in positions where they are likely to be reversed. Point wise, this is foolish. Knowing when to release an opponent is as important as knowing how to ride him.

It is best to stay behind an opponent while riding him and only move up higher after he has been broken down to his stomach. Once on his stomach, he is no longer a threat since he cannot create sufficient force to escape or reverse.

Winning is the primary goal. It isn't everything, but losing isn't anything. In order to win, the wrestler should always play the percentages. His best chance of winning is by wearing his opponent down. This is accomplished by forcing him to carry the burden of both their weights as much as possible.

The best means of immobilizing an opponent is to control his legs. There are three advantages to this type of ride. First, it is difficult for an opponent, who is dependent upon grasping an arm or the head of the top man, to initiate an escape. Secondly, it limits an opponent to attempting only the more risky type of techniques from a position down on the mat. Finally, it keeps an opponent from gaining both a reversal and the position of advantage.

Winning is the objective of all contests. In wrestling, there are two ways of winning. One is to outscore the opponent on points and the other it to pin him. If a wrestler can out-class an opponent to the extent that he can pin him, that is fine, but pinning should not be his immediate objective. His primary objective is to win.

33
Waist Versus Ankle Rides

IN THE TOP OR OFFENSIVE POSITION, CONTROL MUST BE MAINTAINED IN order to keep from losing points. The option of selecting from many techniques exists in achieving this goal. Most of the options fall into one of two broad categories—waist rides and ankle rides. Both categories contain rides of varying degrees of effectiveness. The latter category of ankle rides is, however, the best. Ankle rides are more effective in providing the top man with optimum control.

Riding an opponent's ankle is the least risky means of control. It is the safest and most potent means of immobilizing the bottom man.

A wrestler in the bottom position is, in most cases, dependent upon having his legs free before initiating action toward escaping or reversing. If he cannot free his legs, he cannot stand up. He is limited to attempting escape and reversal techniques from a position down on the mat. Any technique attempted from on the mat is more dangerous in that it has a greater chance of losing points, if countered, than if it were tried from standing. A mistake four inches from the mat is more likely to lose points for the bottom man than one four feet above the mat.

A second advantage of riding an ankle is that the top wrestler is less likely to get reversed and find himself on the bottom. This is explained by the fact that any time he experiences trouble controlling the opponent, he simply has to release the leg. Thus, by permitting the opponent to escape, he loses only one point instead of two. Also, he ends up in a neutral position instead of on the bottom.

If a waist ride is employed, it is not always possible to release the opponent. He can anchor the arm that is around his waist so that it cannot be freed. It then can be used to set up a reversal. Against an ankle ride, however, the best the opponent can do is free himself.

A wrestler should not gamble unless the odds are overwhelmingly in his favor. The odds do not favor riding an opponent with an arm around the waist. There are at least three effective reversal techniques

305 / WAIST VERSUS ANKLE RIDES

that can be employed against a wrestler who rides in this manner. If he pulls the opponent, he can be switched. If he pushes the opponent, he can be rolled. If he does neither, but simply leaves the arm around the waist, he can be whizzered.

One of the best methods of riding an ankle is the leg in lap ride. Not only is it an effective means of controlling an opponent, but it also provides excellent pinning opportunities. The following series of photographs illustrate the leg in lap ride to a pinning situation.

In order to get the opponent's leg into the position shown in photo 126A, it must first be straightened by lifting and pulling back on the ankle. By moving to a position behind the opponent, the leg can be supported on a raised thigh. The hold on the ankle should then be transferred to the upper portion of the leg.

At this point, the top man should shift around to the far side and drop his hand down to pick up the other ankle while gripping the opponent's waist.

Then, by lifting the leg upward, the bottom man is forced onto his back. He is encouraged to turn onto his back by placement of an elbow into his kidney area and the exertion of downward pressure. The bottom man will normally resist turning. However, as the pressure

126A   Leg in Lap. Reaching for opponent's near leg.

increases he will have to turn. A hand should be placed on his chest in anticipation of his making a sudden twisting turn (photo 126B).

At the moment he starts to turn toward the top man, an inside crotch and half nelson combination should be applied (photo 126C).

Another effective ankle ride is illustrated in photos 127A through 128B. The opponent's leg is lifted off the mat and placed on the near thigh. Leverage is gained by stepping between his legs. By keeping the head up, back arched, and driving into him with the hip he can be forced over onto his back.

The far leg lift is a third means of controlling an opponent's leg. It is readily secured when the bottom man sits back on his heels. By reaching across and between his thighs, the hands can be locked around the ankle. Then, by elevating the leg and placing a thigh under the legs, the opponent can be turned onto his shoulders.

In general, it is safest to ride the lower half of the opponent's body and only move up after he has been broken down to his stomach. Once on his stomach, he is no longer a threat since he cannot create sufficient force to execute an effective escape or reversal.

Attempting to control an opponent with a tight waist ride can get the top man into serious trouble. It places him in a position where he is likely to be switched, rolled, or whizzered.

Wrestlers in the bottom position are not, in general, used to having their legs ridden. Consequently, they have become dependent upon being able to grab the top man's arm or head in order to initiate an escape or reversal. This makes riding a leg a very effective means of control.

Riding an opponent's leg is the best method of immobilizing him. It does the most to handicap him since he cannot get very far or move very fast on one leg. If the held leg is lifted, it will almost assuredly place the opponent in an embarrassing position on his back.

126B Lifting opponent's leg thus forcing him onto his back.

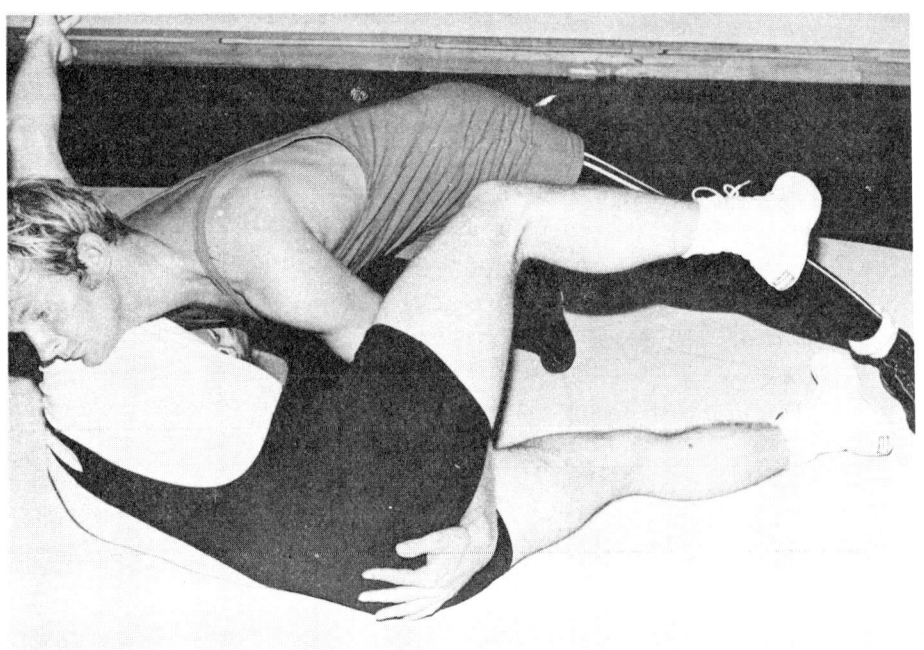

126C Applying a pinning combination.

SYSTEMATIC CHAMPIONSHIP WRESTLING / 308

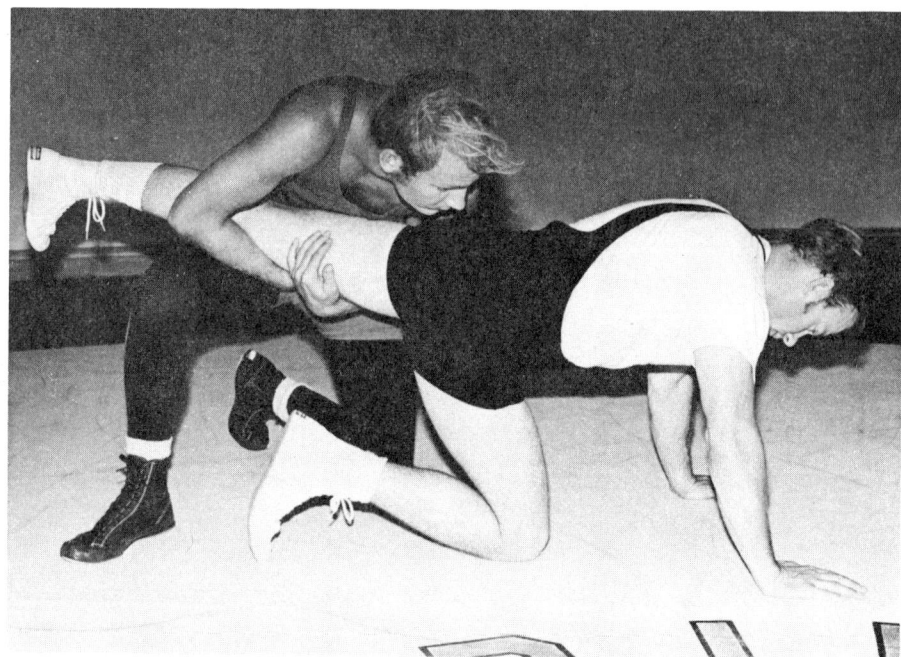

127A   Near Leg Lift to Step Over. Securing a hold on opponent's upper thigh.

127B   Stepping between opponent's legs.

309 / WAIST VERSUS ANKLE RIDES

127C Driving into opponent while applying a pinning combination.

128A Far Leg Lift. Locking hands around opponent's ankle.

128B Lifting the leg thus forcing opponent onto his back.

34
Principles of Leg Wrestling

LEG WRESTLING IS AN ART. ITS UNIQUENESS MAKES IT ONE OF THE MOST effective means of controlling an opponent. A vast number of wrestlers are unaccustomed to being ridden in this manner and know very little about how to effectively cope with it. Consequently, they are less likely to successfully execute an escape or reversal and, thus, their chances of winning are vastly reduced.

Yet, unless it is employed in accordance with certain movement principles, leg wrestling can be instrumental in causing the wrestler who uses it to lose more matches than he wins.

A wrestler, while supported on his hands and knees, is in a strong defensive position. By removing one of his supporting points, he is weakened in that direction. Then, by flattening him to the mat, his chances of escaping or reversing are diminished, his base is destroyed, and his position is vulnerable for the application of a leg. The first principle of successful leg wrestling is to apply the legs only after the opponent has been broken down to the mat.

The smart wrestler plays the percentages as much as possible and gambles only when the situation warrants a calculated risk, or when the odds are overwhelmingly in his favor. He knows that he can get into serious trouble if he attempts to apply his legs while his opponent is in an all-fours position. He avoids applying his legs until after he has his opponent flat on the mat.

Granted, the legs can be applied when an opponent is on all fours. However, the risk of being countered and thus losing points is much greater. Extreme caution must be exercised if the legs are employed before the opponent is flattened. Some of the more common counters against a wrestler who attempts to apply a leg to an opponent in an all fours positions are illustrated in photos 129A through 133C.

Any attempt to work toward a fall once an opponent has been broken down, should not be made too early in the match. The effectiveness of leg wrestling lies in the ability of the top man to wear down

SYSTEMATIC CHAMPIONSHIP WRESTLING / 312

129A Counter #1 to Cross Body Ride. Countering by catching the leg of offensive wrestler with the near arm.

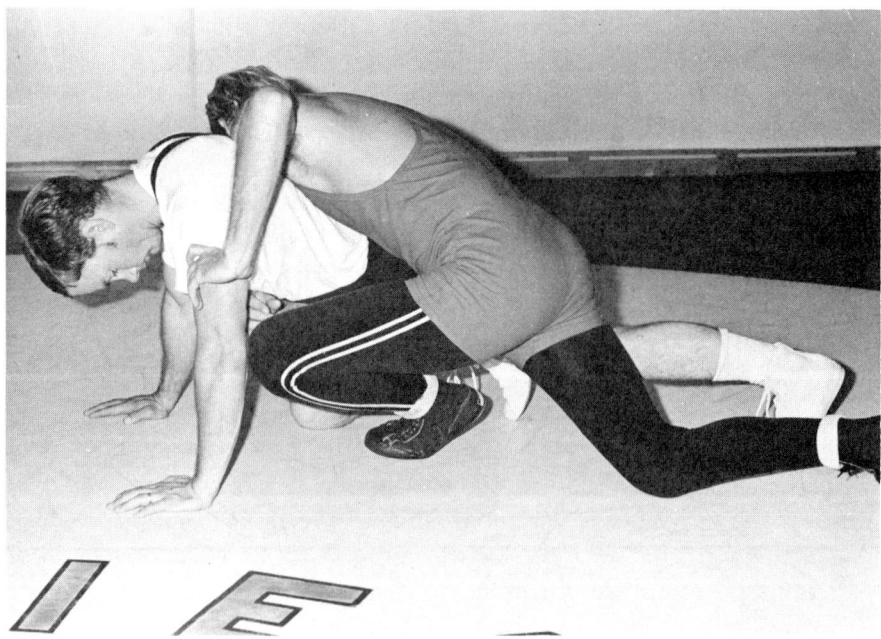

130A Counter #2 to Cross Body Ride. Countering by straightening the leg.

313 / PRINCIPLES OF LEG WRESTLING

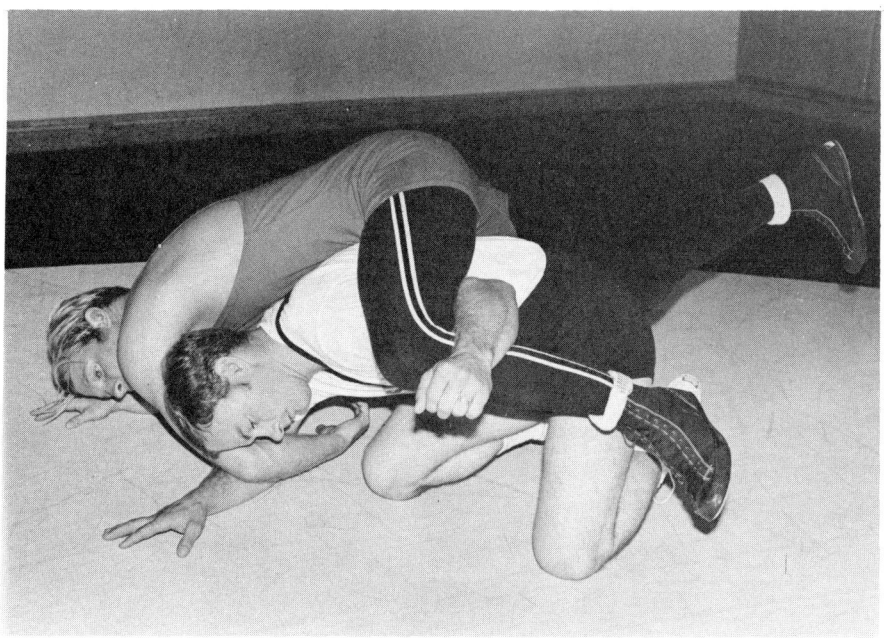

131A Counter #3 to Cross Body Ride. Countering by grasping offensive man's foot while dropping to one side.

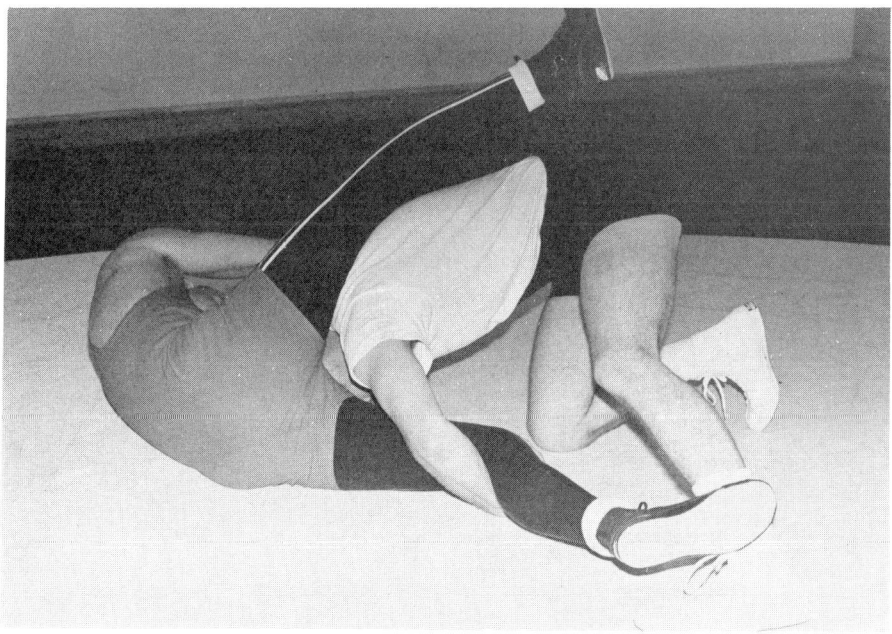

131B Working the arm forward, lifting on the leg, and forcing offensive man over the top.

SYSTEMATIC CHAMPIONSHIP WRESTLING / 314

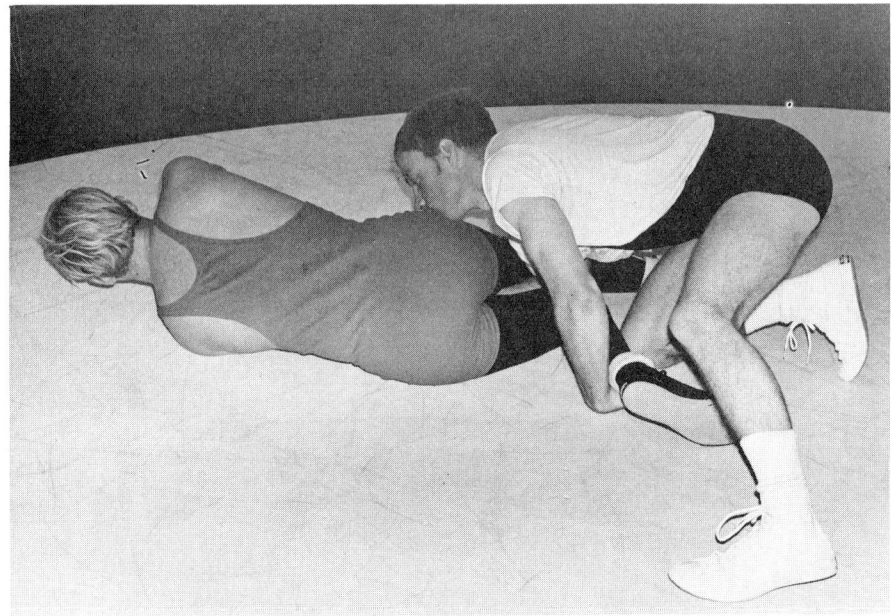

131C Continuing to lift the leg while backing out.

132A Counter to Figure Four Body Scissors. Dropping to one side, working an arm under the leg, and turning toward the offensive wrestler.

315 / PRINCIPLES OF LEG WRESTLING

133A Counter to Crab Ride. Securing a hold on one of offensive man's extended legs.

133B Bringing the captured leg up to the chest.

133C Scooting the buttocks forward and turning the body until an escape is realized.

the opponent by having him support the burden of his weight before going for a fall. The figure four illustrated in photo 134A is effective for wearing down an opponent before applying a pinning combination.

While on top, the offensive wrestler should be concerned with destroying his opponent's base and distributing his weight to his maximum advantage. He should keep the opponent struggling while capitalizing upon opportunities to apply pinning combinations. No more effort than the minimum necessary to maintain control should be exerted. Restricting his expenditure of energy is a must.

The top man should avoid using his legs in a manner that places him in a position other than above an opponent. Any other position is less desirable and more risky. Other positions may put him into precarious situations that are likely to result in his losing control and the position of advantage.

The worst mistake the top man can make when using his legs is failure to remain on top of his opponent. Regardless of the type of leg wrestling employed, it is imperative that he stay above the opponent and never pull him over onto the top.

Only when the top man can make his opponent work harder trying to escape than he has to work to maintain control, will he win. An op-

317 / PRINCIPLES OF LEG WRESTLING

134A Applying a Leg Hold. Applying a figure four body scissors after flattening opponent to a prone position on the mat.

134B Stretching opponent out by arching the back.

SYSTEMATIC CHAMPIONSHIP WRESTLING / 318

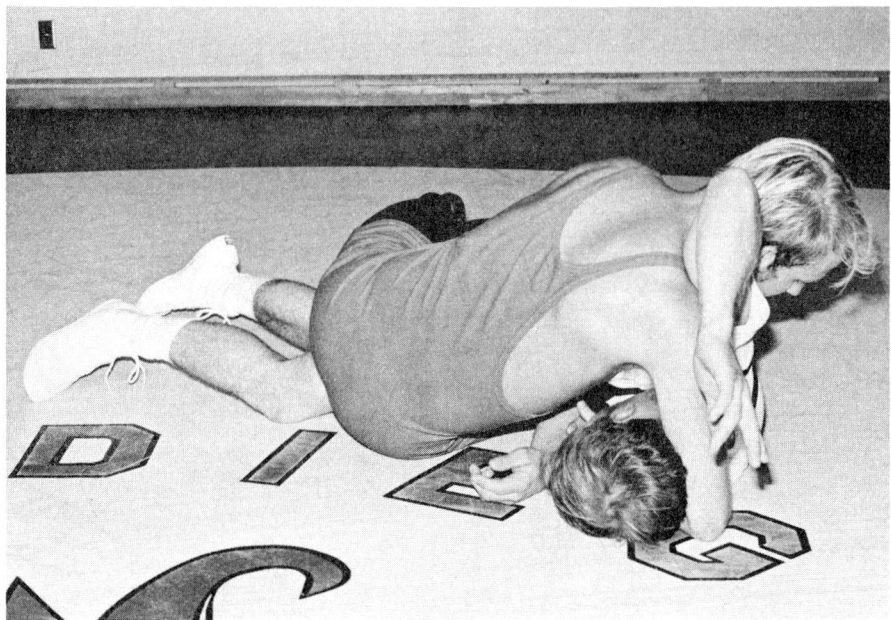

134C Relaxing the pressure slightly in order to allow opponent's body to slip inside the scissors hold.

134D Turning opponent onto his back and retightening the figure four.

319 / PRINCIPLES OF LEG WRESTLING

ponent has to work harder when the man on top stays above and forces him to carry the extra burden of his weight. If the bottom man has to work harder for a long enough period of time, he will be worn down and this will eventually result in his defeat. Photos 135A through 137A illustrate various improper positions in which the top man is not making his opponent carry his weight.

The offensive man must recognize when he is in trouble and likely to lose control. At that time, he must not refuse to release the hold, otherwise he may be reversed and possibly end up on his back. It is important that he know just when to release before chancing the loss of two or more points and the position of advantage. It is best to release the hold before further difficulty is encountered.

There are also principles of leg wrestling that apply to the defensive wrestler. In order to keep the top man from applying a leg, it is important for the defensive wrestler to recover to a hands and knees position without providing an opening for a leg to be inserted. The safest method of recovery is illustrated in photos 138A through 138D.

A wrestler who remains flat on the mat is half-pinned. Once he recovers from his stomach to his hands and knees, he should free his legs, and get to his feet.

135A Improper Position #1. Assuming a very poor position that could prove dangerous if the defensive man gains control.

SYSTEMATIC CHAMPIONSHIP WRESTLING / 320

136A Improper Position #2. Assuming a weak position that is quite tiring for the offensive wrestler.

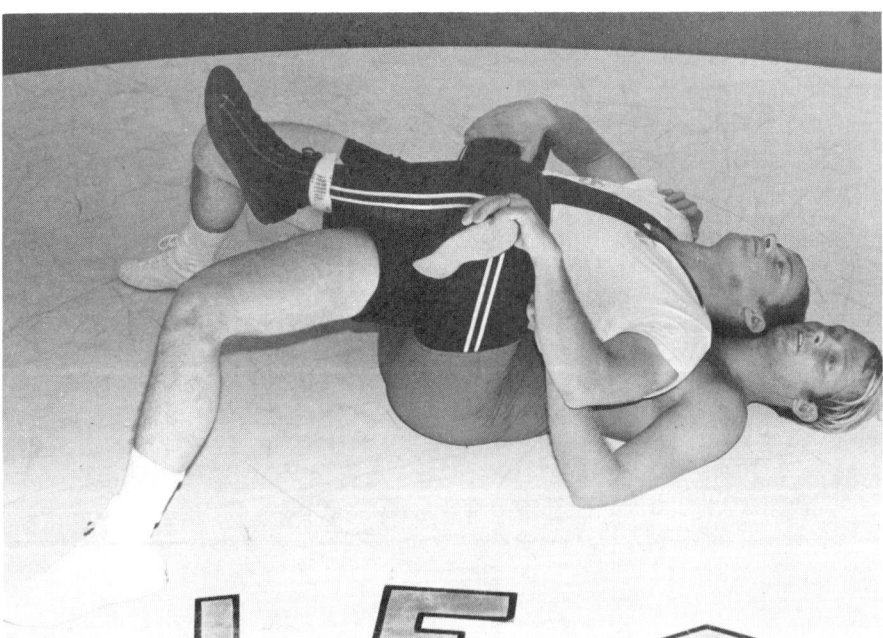

137A Improper Position #3. Assuming a precarious position by failing to stay above opponent.

138A Going From Stomach to Hands and Knees. Getting out of the prone position with a minimum of risk by first moving the arms in close to the body while keeping the head up.

138B Moving one knee toward an elbow by sliding it along the mat and then doing the same with the other knee.

138C Pushing up to a very low crouched position with the elbows on the mat inside the knees.

138D Moving up higher onto the hands and knees by straightening the arms and then finally coming up to standing.

The odds favor the wrestler working from a standing position. When attempting to escape or reverse, more points are lost on a mistake made inches from the mat, while few, if any, are lost on a mistake made several feet above the mat.

While standing, the bottom man has two advantages he does not have while down on the mat. One of these advantages is greater mobility. While standing, he can move much faster than in any position he could assume down on the mat. He is harder to control while standing.

The second distinct advantage is the conservation of energy. While standing, he does not have to carry the top man's weight and is therefore less likely to tire as soon. The energy saved can be employed in extending his efforts to gain an escape or the position of advantage.

A wrestler should never lie on his stomach when he can get to his hands and knees. He should never stay on his hands and knees when he can get to his feet. While standing, it is much easier to move about and much more difficult for the opponent to employ a leg technique.

Bibliography

1. American Association for Health, Physical Education and Recreation. *Weight Training in Sports and Physical Education.* Washington, D.C.: National Education Association, 1962, 175 pp.
2. Astrand, P. O., T. E. Cuddy, B. Saltin, and J. Stenberg. Cardiac Output During Submaximal and Maximal Work. *J. of App. Physio.,* 19 (March 1964): 268–274.
3. Camaione, David N. and Kenneth G. Tillman. *Wrestling Methods.* New York: Ronald Press Co., 1968, 268 pp.
4. Councilman, James E. *The Science of Swimming.* Englewood Cliffs, New Jersey: Prentice-Hall, Inc., 1968.
5. Davis, Elwood C., Gene A. Logan, and Wayne C. McKinney. *Biophysical Values of Muscular Activity.* Dubuque, Iowa: Wm. C. Brown Co., 1965.
6. Dratz, John P., Manly Johnson, and Terry McCann. *Winning Wrestling.* Englewood Cliffs, New Jersey: Prentice-Hall, Inc., 1966, 195 pp.
7. Hoffman, Bob. *Weight Training for Athletes.* New York: Ronald Press Co., 1961, 216 pp.
8. Kapral, Lt. Frank S. *Coach's Illustrated Guide to Championship Wrestling.* Englewood Cliffs, New Jersey: Prentice-Hall, Inc., 1964, 276 pp.
9. Karvoven, M. J., E. Kentala, and O. Mustala. The Effects of Training on Heart Rate. *Ann. Med. Exper. Fenn.* 35 (1957): 307–315. Cited in Kasch, F. W., and Boyer, J. L., *Adult Fitness Principles and Practices.* Greeley, Colorado: All American Prod. and Publ., 1968, p. 29.
10. ———. Effects of Vigorous Activity on the Heart. *Work and the Heart,* ed. by Rosenbaum, F. F. & E. L. Belknap. New York: Paul Hoeber, 1959.
11. ———. Effects of Vigorous Exercise on the Heart. *Work and the Heart.* F. R. Rosenbaum and E. L. Belknap (eds). New York: Paul B. Hoeber, Inc., 1959.
12. Keith, Art. *Complete Guide to Championship Wrestling.* West Nyack, New York: Parker Publishing Co., Inc., 1968, 241 pp.
13. Murray, James A. and Peter Karpovich. *Weight Training in Athletics.* Englewood Cliffs, New Jersey: Prentice-Hall, Inc., 1956, 214 pp.

14. O'Shea, John Patrick. *Scientific Principles and Methods of Strength Fitness.* Reading, Massachusetts: Addison-Wesley Publishing Co., 1969, 165 pp.
15. Rasch, Philip J. "Endurance Training for Athletes." *Journal of Association for Physical and Mental Rehabilitation.* Nov.–Dec., 1956.
16. ——— and Walter Kroll. *What Research Tells the Coach About Wrestling.* Washington, D.C.: A.A.H.P.E.R., 1964.
17. ——— and Walter Kroll. *What Research Tells the Coach About Wrestling.* Washington, D.C.: National Education Association, 1964, 56 pp.
18. Sclye, Hans. *The Stress of Life.* New York: McGraw-Hill Book Co., 1956.
19. Steinhaus, Arthur. *Toward an Understanding of Health and Physical Education.* Dubuque, Iowa: Wm. C. Brown Co., 1963.